In the Clearing Stands A Doorman and A Fighter By His Trade

By Steve Young

A CIP catalogue record for this book is available from the British Library
Printed and bound in Great Britain.

ISBN 9798730062269
ISBN

Please note: The theoretical information and physical techniques outlined in this book are for information purposes only. The authors and the publishers cannot accept any responsibility for any proceedings or prosecutions brought or instituted against any person or body as a result of the misuse of any theoretical information or physical techniques described in this book or any loss, injury or damage caused thereby.

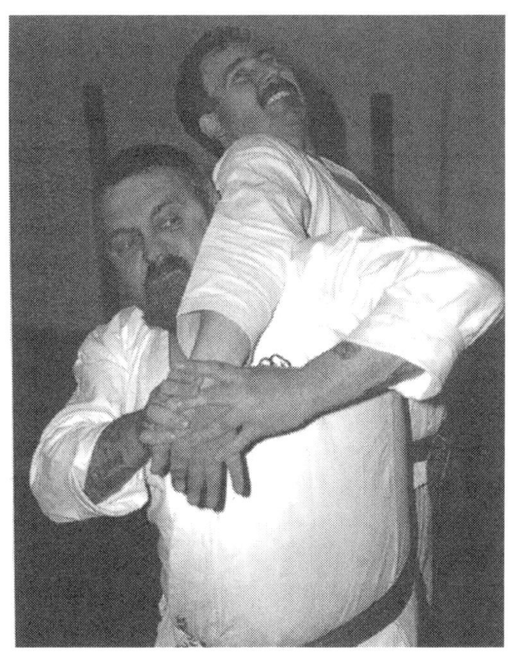

I dedicate this book to Warrior Gary James Spiers 1943 – 2001

May the Maori Gods of War watch over his soul.
Steve Young

When I was in my teens and just started training within karate, to right through my career in martial arts I never once dreamt that I would write a book with my all-time hero Terry O'Neil (World karate champion and voted greatest martial artist of all time in the world-circulating *Martial Arts* magazine) writing the foreword. But he actually has here. This man, known as "The Hard Man of Shotokan", is a true genuine warrior by the very definition of the word and one of the most gracious gentlemen I have ever met. My salute to him reaches the stars.

Steve Young

Me and Terry

FOREWORD BY TERRY O'NEILL

Over the years I've been both privileged and pleased to be asked to write forewords to a number of different books. While considering this an honour, I'm aware that it also carries with it a certain responsibility – by providing a foreword to a book, one is essentially endorsing its content. For this reason, I've always insisted that I see a proof copy before actually agreeing to put pen to paper … until this one!

Because the author, a fellow martial artist, has been a good pal of mine for many years – and because of the subject matter of this book – bouncers, nightclubs, and violence – are not unfamiliar to me, I said yes to him, before seeing the manuscript. Once I'd realised my error, I had an anxious period contemplating how I'd get out of my verbal commitment should this book – for any reason – be one that I'd not wish to put my name to. Needless to say, I wasn't scared. OK, Steve is a well-trained and undeniably a tough nut … however as the saying goes, I've done a bit myself!

But I'd given him my word … I need not have worried. *In the Clearing Stands a Doorman and a Fighter by His Trade* proved to be not only well written, entertaining, and informative, but also surprisingly humorous, and I have no hesitation at all in whole-heartedly recommending it!

the Red Triangle team who were National Team Champions on thirteen occasions.

Terry was also Captain of the British All Styles Squad who made history in defeating Japan, their first ever loss, in 1972 in Paris. Terry was also a member of the British Shotokan Team who went on to beat the Japanese and won the World Championships in California.

A senior member of the KUGB since its establishment, Terry is also an International Referee and is one of the KUGB Grading Examiners.

He was also an A-list actor appearing alongside Arnold Schwarzenegger, Michael Cain, and Sean Connery to mention just a few and he also appeared on television probably the most well-known in *The Governor*.

Yes, the *great* Terry O'Neill … the story goes on and on, but that's another book.

absolutely overwhelm the whole of the city. It's surreal; the streets become rivers of sick, with the odd body strewn on the pavement every few hundred yards. Many customers I speak to prefer Liverpool or Manchester for an evening out as it's far less violent.

We also have a large army barracks just on the edge of town called The Dale. It's full of young, fit, lively squaddies being trained to kill people. Need I say anymore on that one?

The town attracts groups and parties from neighbouring towns, such as Birkenhead, Ellesmere Port, Crewe, Liverpool, and North Wales. Birkenhead was once regarded nationally as Britain's most violent city.

Even the Great Gary Spiers, who finished his days off here, and had worked within the physical security sector in most of the major cities around the globe, described Chester as one of the most confrontational places he'd ever worked in.

So, the doors had to be geared up accordingly.

Here, I recall some amazing stories of violence and dark humoured moments in the not so distant past, when, if you worked the doors, you had to be able to *do it*.

PREFACE

I've worked the doors for over twenty-five years, mostly in and around Chester.

This town, to anyone who doesn't know it too well, may conjure up thoughts of a quaint, antique, sleepy, old Roman city, full of lovely, rich old pensioners.

Well, nothing could be further from the truth.

We have the biggest council estate in Europe, called Blacon. Its handle on the national CB radio band is WigWam, as it's said to be full of savages. Although that name must have been given by people who've only heard the scary rumours of the place, as it's not strictly true. I have relatives and many friends there but there is an estate nearby, the Lache, which is almost as big, and equally tasty, with a high proportion of hard men).

The centre of Chester is purely a place of entertainment. At weekends it attracts large groups of pub and club goers from all over the region. The town, Chester City, was voted the north-west's favourite city to visit.

We also have a famous racetrack called The Roodee, which is a favourite of the jockeys and the TV pundits alike.

We have at least two race meetings a month which attract literally thousands of racegoers (I use that term very loosely) who

INTRODUCTION

The stories I tell here are about me and some of the fantastic men I've worked with. Doormen of the old school. A pretty much extinct breed of tough, hard, capable men who, in those days, had to be and look harder than anyone who entered your venue. That was the whole idea and your sole purpose.

You were purely there for the nasty people, dealing with them as they chose to put it to you.

We used to say we were like magnified mirrors to them, anything they did or tried to do to us or others, they would get back bigger. If they went up a gear, we'd go up fuckin' two.

The only rule was, if you behaved and were respectful to the place and the other customers, you would have a good night. If your intentions were purely to be a cunt, you would be dealt with like one.

This bears no resemblance to how the job functions today. So, as something of a tribute to the Pavement Warriors I've met and worked with, I respectfully pen our stories here.

From left to right – Big Billy, me, Big Tony, and Big Mike.

To put this picture in perspective I'm 6 foot!

CHAPTER ONE

My Introduction to the Doors

I was in my early thirties when I had my first chance meeting with the famous Gary Spiers.

Gary, for those who've never heard of him, was one of the highest respected martial artists in the world.

He was half Maori, towering well over six foot, with a twenty-five stone powerhouse of a frame. He fled to Japan from New Zealand following a fight with a squaddie after he bit off his ear. He told me he was worried about leaving any evidence, so he swallowed it.

During his eight years in Japan, he continued his martial arts practice, training at one of the top GoJu dojos, run by one of the highest respected GoJu masters in the world, Morio Higaonna. Higaonna soon took a shine to Gary, even putting him up in his house. Gary soon rose through the ranks there, eventually becoming an instructor to non-Japanese visiting students.

It was in that position he met a high-ranking student from England by the name of Terry O'Neill. They became immediate friends.

I took him through to the dojo where he introduced himself in the same manner. My students totally shit themselves. I remember him apologising for his language saying, *I'm sorry if my swearing might offend anyone, but I learnt fackin English from you cants.*

In the reverence of a martial arts dojo, you would never ever hear that type of talk, but we all absolutely warmed to him and all learnt some devastating street related techniques that morning…

I knew then that I wanted to train more with this man and get to know him better, and I did. For the next four and a half years, he lived with me in my house.

When I first started to get to know Gary, I was married, but totally out of the blue, she dropped the biggest bombshell I'd ever experienced in my life and told me that, after eighteen years of marriage, she was leaving me. It shattered my life to pieces and brought me close to suicide. Gary was a tower of strength to me and, along with my now fiancée, Lin, saved my life.

When my wife moved out, (to live with a friend of mine – or should I say ex fuckin' friend) Gary moved in with me and soon had me working on the doors with him. He'd come over from Liverpool to Chester to do some security work for a millionaire builder. He worked at that during day and took a few doors on in town to be active at night. He hadn't been in Chester long before he was running the largest door company in town.

My first night working the doors with him was at the newly opened Irish themed bar, Ryan's. It was a mid-weeknight when they didn't usually have door staff on, but the local radio station was there and as a precaution to any silliness, they'd asked Gary to put some security on.

I remember him saying to me that it would be dead and be a nice easy start for me. Yep, that old kiss of death … famous last words…

Part way through the live broadcast, a group of two couples started to argue quite loudly. It transpired (and being picked up live on air) that there had been some cross infidelity between them. It soon developed into a violent fight between all four with more and more sordid details being inadvertently aired on the local radio. That is until they fell into the equipment and brought an impromptu halt to the program. We eventually got them out, but the gentleman I was dragging out was proving something of a problem as one of the ladies (I use that term very loosely) was walloping him repeatedly with her handbag all the way to the door.

At the end of the night, we had a staff drink or three and a good laugh about it as Gary recalled several similar experiences. He'd seen it all, and it all sounded such an exciting, colourful world, and what with him telling me how well I'd coped that night, I agreed to do a regular Friday and Saturday there. What could possibly go wrong? I would be working with the main man, *and* I was a second-degree karate black belt…

Well, working with the main man held credibility, but my martial arts experience and training, all learnt in the safety of a controlled environment of the dojo (training hall), proved not fully *Pavement Worthy*.

I soon had to admit this to Gary, knowing full well he was spotting it and to his great amusement. So we started training together most days…

I still jointly owned a small bakery with my wife. But as she'd left me, I thought it only right to leave her to run the fuckin' thing on

her own, leaving me clear to train with Gary in the day and work with him at night putting it all into practice.

Me (second from right), Gary (second from left), assisting on one of his seminars with two of his solicitors, Robbie & Mark

Gary loved his work; he was born for it. He used to say, Don't look at it so much as work, but more as practice for you, Stevey, and don't hate these cunts for being cunts (or cants, as he would pronounce it) they're keeping us in work, so just see them as live targets.

This, I might add, was in the good old days before the game got regulated by the government (wrongly, in my opinion, which I'll elaborate fully on in the conclusion of this book) and before everyone got the *Where there's blame, there's a claim* virus. These days, no matter how deserving they are, you bang someone and they're on their fuckin' mobile to the solicitor before they hit the ground … bless!

Gary, as I've said, was a high-graded karate martial artist in the style of GoJu Ryu, but when I met him and started training with him, he explained to me he'd updated a system of fighting arts to cope more with modern-day, contemporary violence which he called Applied Karate. It was great to train and learn these very relevant techniques. I later learnt it had come about with much collaboration with his senior student, Richie Herbert.

The story is that Gary had gone on one of his walkabouts. He'd often be away for long periods abroad on minding or bodyguarding jobs. On this occasion he left Richie in charge. Richie, at that time, was experiencing the same problems and doubts I was in relating and transferring his training to the harsh reality of the nightclub door. So he started extra training in other fighting systems, learning the best bits from them, and incorporated them into his classes. On Gary's unannounced return, Richie explained what he'd done and to his surprise, and relief, Gary fully embraced the changes and additions.

These other techniques Gary recognised as he had trained in most of the styles in their country of origin. So with Gary's backing, fine tuning, and a good few additions, it now carried the credibility to be recognised as a new style of martial art, which was christened Applied Karate.

This style became famous, and Gary was being asked to conduct many one-day seminars throughout the country to huge classes from all styles, a lot of them I assisted him with.

Most of my evenings were now tied up, so I passed my karate club to my two senior students, but I started, with Gary's approval, a Sunday class teaching the new techniques I'd learnt, using bags, pads, and dummy weapons. It became extremely popular attracting ex-students of mine and students from other styles wanting to participate in some reality training, local lads wanting to improve their self-defence capabilities, and most importantly, other doormen.

Me with three world champions left to right – Lance Lewis, me, Sean Viera, and Ronny Green

It came to a point that Gary would check the register and if any of our doormen hadn't attended a Sunday class without a good sick note, they wouldn't work the following week.

As he took more doors on in town, the bigger the classes became.

It's a stipulation I still make today, and even with the tight constraints of the new government vetting procedure, I insist all

doormen working for us must have a good background in some form of fighting art, unlike the majority of the new style of doormen I see, who look like squirts with little or no capability.

I got talking to one such doorman recently, a scrawny little fucker all kitted out in his new doorman's gear. He looked like

Sooty's fuckin' wand. I asked him if he did any martial arts or boxing, he replied, *Na, just a bit of gardening*.

For fuck's sake, gardening! This pillock wouldn't have been able to put the fuckin' cat out, but there he was with his new shiny badge, in charge of hundreds of people's safety.

There was a huge cinema just around the corner from where we were working that was being converted into a two-thousand capacity nightclub, to be called Brannigans. All the local – and a lot of national – security companies had tendered for this venue, but Gary had already secured it with the allegiance of a squeaky clean, very legal, company from North Wales run by a man called Paul Blakemore. He fronted the operation, but it was manned mostly by Gary's men. His top men. Paul did have some damn good lads though.

One of note was a kid called Gerite who was to front the venue as head doorman. He was absolutely perfect for the position as with the attention Brannigans was expecting, and did get, from the press, the police, and the many famous customers it attracted, he would be just the man. Articulate, tall, dark, and handsome with a striking resemblance to Clark Gable (yeah! ya can hate the fucker from his mere description with abject jealousy!). The guy was OK and could well have a go.

But the bollocks of the operation were Gary's men, led by Richie, closely assisted by a highly respected guy called Eddy Lucas.

The venue required eighteen doormen, all of whom were right out of the top drawer, and all of whom I'd worked with at some point.

Some of the more, shall we say *colourful* stories from these times, I'll tell later in the book, along with other more grizzly, violent, and humorous stories…

CHAPTER TWO

Highly Capable Men of Courage, Warriors of the Door Who Had the Fear Gene Missing from Their Physiological Make-up

The Green Machine

Michal Green, or Greenie as he was better known, had to be the scariest person ever to walk God's green earth. Anyone who met him will totally agree with that statement.

He was naturally bald but had thick waves of flesh on his head down to the base of his neck, had piercing eyes with heavy rolls of flesh where eyebrows should have been, standing around six foot six, and weighing in at well over twenty stone. Well, if this fucker said it was Christmas, you'd start singing carols!

I first met Greenie shortly after he got out of prison.

Gary arranged to meet him at this trucker's café. He and Gary went back many years, doing high-level body guarding to many A-list stars, including Michael Jackson, Tina Turner, and Joe Cocker.

We arrived, and I spotted him instantly, exactly like the description I'd been given, but jaw droopingly scarier in the flesh.

He and Gary embraced, and we were introduced. Gary asked him how prison and his cellmate were. He replied, in a deep growling tone, *Yeah, he was OK, no one we know, just some little fucker. I never shagged him, just ate his dinners*.

Gary got Greenie work in one of the nightclubs we did called Blimpers. It was a bit seedy and could get quite tasty. Yeah, a square peg in a square hole there. But also, at that time, Gary was getting busier and busier, so now that I was starting to get the swing of things, he got Greenie to work with me on Friday nights until we closed at eleven thirty. Then he'd do what we call a *walk over* and go on to the nightclub. On Saturday nights Gary had me working with this other guy called Alan, from the neighbouring town who I'd met a few times briefly but had heard loads about. He was that town's hard man. His title spread across quite a few other neighbouring towns, a man I'll go further into detail about later, but needless to say, I was left in damn safe company.

My first night with the Green Machine I watched him park up opposite the bar and slowly struggle to get his huge bulk out of his car. It looked like someone had pulled the cord on a giant inflatable dingy. I was quite worried about working with him, but from the time he got halfway across the road to the time he left to go to Blimpers, I never stopped laughing.

The stories he told me, the way he was with people, just blew me away and he was the very first person to talk irreverently about Gary. I went home that night with my abs killing me from pain through all the laughing.

He said to me, *You do the talking, lad. I'll just come in if it warms up*. Yeah, that's how it worked. We'd get undesirable lads (or potential victims, as he'd like to refer to them), I would refuse them entry and most often they would get arsey.

There was a point they would get to, probably one step away from violence, when Greenie would make his appearance from out of the shadows like a giant scary mask, zooming in on you out of a dark sky, where he'd say, in a long, drawn-out gravelly voice, *Are you sure?!*

That usually did the trick. It fuckin' did with me. Every time he said it to someone, I'd shit myself!

He soon moved across from Southport to Ellesmere Port and we started to become great friends. Me and my girl, Lin, met his wife and to our surprise she was this sweet little dark thing. He saw the look on my face and smiled. He said to me later, *That shocked you didn't it, lad? Well, ya should have seen me first wife, Godzilla*! I did meet her years later and boy was he was right!

Well, the four of us started to go out together. I really got to love this fella. He was fantastic company with a huge heart, and he became massively popular with all the other doormen too.

Where he moved to was right near where I held my Sunday training classes. When we'd finished training, we would all go on to my local pub for a well-earned Sunday session. It wasn't long before he got onto this and he would turn up at the club just as we were finishing. I would take him to the pub in my car and afterwards we'd get him a taxi home.

The lads loved him, as after a few pints, he would tell his stories, even the locals would be pulling their chairs up to hear his tales.

I remember one Sunday, this scrawny, horrible barmaid called Shelly (we all referred to her as *Shitty*) who had made it plain she disliked us all going in there, said to Greenie in a sneering manner as he stood there with his huge heavy build, *Oh, so you do the martial arts too, do you*?

She made the mistake of being on our side of the bar.

Greenie zoomed in on her, putting his arms either side of her on the wall, pinning her there, and said in a tone usually reserved for the nightclub, *Yes, love. I'm a black belt* – he paused for a few seconds as his face turned in to a granite-like scowl – *in fuckin' stool throwin'*. She slithered down under one of his arms and shot up the stairs like a rat up a drainpipe. The whole pub was in fits of laughter. We never saw her again that afternoon.

There are so many amazing stories about this man I could fill two books with them, but I'll recall a few here that are more printable.

The Baboon with Connections

Greenie used to work every weekend evening until the early hours, leaving him little time in the day for his family. Even mid-week evenings, when he wasn't working, Gary would have him out on safari – when you go out to deal with someone who's crossed you.

His wife constantly nagged him to spend more time with the family. This one Saturday morning, she woke him up saying, *Come on, Mick, get dressed. You're going on safari*. He said, *No one's told me of any mither*. She replied, *No, you idiot*! *A real safari, I've arranged for us and the kids to go to Knowsley Safari Park.*

So off they go, everything going swimmingly until they reached the baboon enclosure.

Anyone who has ever been here will know how they climb all over your vehicle and how it can get quite scary.

I remember Greenie telling this story one Sunday in the local to a large spell-bound audience. He'd coloured it up a bit, but the main plot of this story is absolutely true as verified by all the passengers.

I'll try to tell it as he recalled it to us.

As they drove through the compound, the baboons started climbing on and diving all over the car. The wife and kids were all nervously laughing until the large alpha male leapt onto the car with a rocking thud then started to bend the aerial back and forth. Greenie said, *I wasn't too happy with the other fuckers crawling all over it, but this cunt was taking the piss! So, I reached into the glove compartment, grabbed me brass (knuckle duster), and got out and chinned it...*

I've heard that baboons are, pound for pound, one of the strongest animals on the planet. I was astounded to think he'd got out of the vehicle, put his brass on, and dusted the monkey without a second thought, but that was typical of the man.

So off they drive, everyone now very silent, until his young son said, *Dad, that monkey you just knocked out has come to and just ran off.*

Yeah, said Greenie. *He'll have gone back to his mates.*

It certainly had. Moments later his young son said, *Dad, that monkey you knocked out has come back with his mates.*

Greenie said, *I looked back, and the fucker had sorted a call-out! I must have weighed in the boss! They were jumping on every car and the boss one would look in and shake its head and go* nah, that's not him, *each time getting nearer and nearer, eventually getting to mine. I put me baseball cap on quickly in an attempt to disguise myself, but it was too late, it had ID'd me.*

It spread across the windscreen, rolled its lips back to expose its giant Dracula teeth as if to say, these are for you, ya cunt!

Then all hell broke loose as they started to kick, punch, and bash lumps out of the car. I had no alternative but to swerve full lock out the queue and speed off down this dirt track.

Next thing I can hear someone shouting on a mega horn, I looked behind me and saw it was the white hunter Land Rover chasing me as well. I thought fuck me! How well connected is this fuckin' monkey? Coz I know this crew have guns.

It was OK though, as it had all been seen in the office on CCTV and they'd sent one of the rangers out to rescue us.

Once out of the baboon compound, we decided to get straight off before they run the camera back and saw me committing a section 18 on the fucker.

Fuckin' day out with the kids?! I'd rather do a house rush on one of the Mafia!

Talking of house rushes, I once asked him if he'd ever been the recipient of one, after hearing his many stories of his leading roles in said activity – a house rush is where a group of people visit someone who has crossed them, leaving them not quite as they found them.

Yes, lad, once, he said. *It was when I was living with my first wife. This one night I was woken by the creak of my stairs and I knew immediately it was more than one person.*

I asked him if he was hurt very badly and to my absolute amazement, he replied matter-of-factly, *No, lad. Fortunately, I managed to pull the wife on top of me in the nick of time and all I got caught with was a few minor hand injuries.*

I then asked how about his wife. *Was she injured much at all?*

Oh fuckin' hell! Of course, lad! They were well tooled up, fuck yeah, she was in hospital for weeks.

I couldn't stop laughing! More at the way he'd told me, as if it was a normal reaction. He told me, unsurprisingly, that his relationship and marriage to her very soon after fizzled out into divorce…

One other story I can mention that's printable is where he and a security team put together by Gary were working on a large outdoor music festival. During the day it was more a kind of country fete with side stalls and exhibitions with the evening being the music concert come rave. Gary, Greenie, and a few of the lads patrolled the daytime events just as a presence. They weren't expecting any trouble in the day apart from boredom. He told me it wasn't until he noticed a group of young lads congregating around an enclosure that had several rare breeds of Vietnamese pot-bellied pigs in, one of which was about twenty stone.

I walked over, and they were all starring at the big one that was just lying there. I looked and couldn't see the attraction, so I said, All right, lads. *They never answered or even looked at me, so I said,* That pig's not doing much is it*? To which one replied,* It fuckin will in a minute, mate, I've just fed it thirty-six quid's worth of Es. *Just then the pig went completely berserk, crashing through its enclosure fence, and proceeded to run amok through the fete.*

It was total chaos with people diving for their kids and stalls being knocked down.

Greenie did paint a very vivid picture when recalling a story, I could see it all in my mind's eye and was uncontrollably laughing at the way in which he was telling me. I asked him if the pig was OK in the end.

Oh yes, fine, lad, it killed itself when it ran into a traction engine, but we never caught them bleedin' lads.

He said there was another funny incident that day when he and Gary noticed Geoff Capes World Champion Shot-Putter and World's Strongest Man Champion was there doing strength demonstrations.

Geoff ran a large security firm and months earlier he was commissioned to remove Gary and his team from a large nightclub in the north-west as the owner suspected they had a scam going on concerning the entrance fee.

Gary and his men had to leave that job as he suspected the police may have also been involved, but they didn't go quietly. Tempers got frayed, and a scuffle ensued where Gary reportedly slashed Geoff across the arse with a razor knife.

At the fete, Geoff was showing how many bricks in a line he could pick up by squashing them together, then inviting members of the audience to have a go.

Gary always used to greet people with the same phrase, *How the fack are ya, Dig?* in a very pronounced Kiwi accent, it was his signature.

Greenie told me how, when Gary spotted Geoff, he managed to creep up behind him just as he'd lifted ten bricks up in a line. He whispered in his ear the famous, *How the fack are ya, Dig?* as he drew a felt pen across his arse. Greenie said he saw Geoff's eyes double in size and the bricks go everywhere. He said Gary just strutted off laughing…

I did ask Gary about this and he confirmed it adding, *Yes, I did, Dig, with a big black felt pen. Do ya know, Dig, he's got an arse two yards fackin wide.*

If I ever run into Geoff Capes, I'd love to ask him about that one.

Alan the Mallet

Alan Millet, though he was referred to as the Mallet, was the man who Gary had working with me on Saturday nights at the Irish Bar. Someone who I became great friends with and still am to this day.

He was an ex pro-heavyweight boxer who, in my opinion, is the very definition of the ultimate doorman. Polite – well, until politeness ceased to work – a talented street fighter, smart, good physical presence, trained every day, and masses of street credibility.

I was told by the local boxing coach that in his day as a pro boxer, he was the hottest property in the north-west.

Boxers, I've found, were the most capable on the doors when it came down to the physical as most fights in our job start in, or within, the confined space of what we call the shake hands distance, where any fancy moves can't be deployed. Which I can personally confirm!

Alan was one of the reasons Gary came up to our neck of the woods as just before he was commissioned to work for this millionaire builder up here. Gary and his team were brought up to take over the security of a privately owned nightclub just out of town called The Glider by its owner. Alan was working at a nearby club called The Waverley and he'd heard that the new head doorman at The Glider was chatting shit about the lads at The Waverley saying they were useless and none of them could fight. So, he phoned up the club and asked to speak to him. Alan asked him about this to which he replied, *Well, if people are saying I said it, I must have said it, pal*, and put the phone down on him.

Alan was furious and got someone to drive him there immediately, telling no one where he was going.

The story goes: He walked into the club and asked, *Who's the head doorman here*? Foolishly, this tit came forward saying, *That would be me, can I help you*? Alan replied, *Yep, I'm Alan from The Waverley*, then smashed him to fuckin jam. There were three other doormen there that night and they all got weighed in, weighed in badly.

I asked Gary about this and he said, *Fackin' hell, yes, Dig. When I was called in, me and Richie went there the following night for a meeting, and everyone was sporting a serious injury. All the doormen looked like they'd been through a food processor. Even the cloakroom attendant and glass collectors had black eyes and twisted noses. I couldn't believe one man was responsible for this carnage. It looked more like the work of a call-out with Rottweilers. The owner asked us to take over the security of The Glider there and then and could I go round and have a word with this Alan. I thought, ya fackin right, I'll be havin' a word with him, I've got to have this cant workin' for us.*

Years later, Alan and Greenie met up via Gary and ended up working at the same place for a while and became good friends.

Alan told me when they first met, Greenie said, *Oy, aren't you that bloke that was brought down to sort out the mither over that Glider club place*? Alan told me, *I shuffled my right leg behind myself to give less of a target ready to defend myself as I wasn't sure how this man was about to react. I said, yes, Mick that was me, mate.* Then Greenie gave off this big beaming, almost childlike grin and said, as he put his hand on Alan's shoulder, *Hey, lad, you were responsible for getting us a lot of work. We did that Glider club for ages on serious wedge, (money) until one night we had a bad tear up with a little local crew and had to all get off an' lie low. But yeah, you got us all some good wages. We did Friday, Saturday, and*

Sunday, all on over the going rate and when we fancied doing the odd night in the week, when the place functioned as just a bar with no security, we'd get someone to phone in an' say, This is Alan Millet, I'm on me way over, *seconds later we'd get a panicking phone call off the manager to come in.*

The trouble with the little local crew Greenie referred to was, when a group of lads, who were some sort of deal in the area were in the club this one night being really shitty. To their horror, the door lads got them out quite easily. Once they'd been put out, they began to hurl stuff at the door and kick cars in the car park.

Greenie told me, *There was quite a few of them, so we all went outside and got it on with them. It was a complete free-for-all, but during the melee, lad, I noticed the manager, Dave, cycling up to the club. He'd been out on his eight hundred quid mountain bike training. He stopped short of the club, nearly skidding into the rumble as he fell off. He quickly got to his feet and scampered into the safety of the club. It was great, lad, as right in the thick of it, I managed to crawl through the melee, grab the bike, and stash it in me van.*

I laughed till I cried, when he told me that one. It sounded like something off a slapstick silent movie.

He went on to say, *The downside of that night, lad, was we gave those lads such a bad kicking we all had to get off from there and lie low. Spiers went crazy, which made me laugh, lad, cause if he was there that night, we would have had to leave the bleedin' country*!

But getting back to Alan. Again I could fill two books with stories of this man. He's absolute folklore in his and the neighbouring towns. I've worked with him in a few places for quite some time now and I've never, ever known him not to be able to deal with any situation he fronted. I'm honoured and proud to be able to call this man a friend.

There is one other story of this man I found very amusing and feel worthy to recall here.

Alan had turned up for work at The Waverly Club, (the Waverly Club? It should have been called The OK Corral). The club was near the docks in Ellesmere Port, and you would often get sailors in from all nationalities. One evening, a Royal Navy ship had docked on its way to Barrow-in-Furness. Three sailors, (field gunners) had come into the club just before the doormen had started and had walked through without paying. The manager had asked them to pay or leave but they told him where to go and when he told them the door staff would be on duty soon, they burst into fits of laughter.

Alan was the first doorman to arrive. The manager raced over to tell him of the situation and suggested he hung on until the other doormen got there as one of the sailors was huge and being very arsey.

Alan said, *It's OK, I'll have a quick word with them*, as he walked up to them, the big one said, *Hey, sonny, we've just told the other prick to fuck off, it's a fuckin' dive here, so we're not paying no fuckin' entrance fee*. Alan said, *No, mate, it don't work like that, pay or drink up and go*. The guy slowly took a sip of his drink, looked at his glass before putting it down, then launched a big, swinging right hook. The other doormen had just got in and ran over, but it was too late. Alan slipped under the fist and fired a multiple shot combination into the bullying twat. The other sailors didn't want to know, and they carried the comatose body out.

A few days later, the manager of The Waverley phoned Alan to say he'd been contacted by a lawyer. The sailors were pressing charges and suggested that he contacted his solicitor, which he quickly did. The solicitor asked Alan how badly he'd hit him. Alan replied that it was a few *light blows*, just enough to subdue him. The solicitor thought all should be fine. They'd just have to wait for the doctor's report, but it should be all above board as it was a government navy doctor. *I'll call you when I've received the report.* A few days later, the solicitor phoned Alan and asked him to come in as he'd received the doctor's report.

Alan told me as soon as he walked into the office and saw the look on the solicitor's face, he knew things were not good. The solicitor said, *Alan, we can't use the doctor's report in our defence*, and he began to read it out aloud. *I've personally known this sailor for many years, when he walked into my surgery I completely and totally did not recognise him. It was only after several minutes of conversation that I realised who it was I'd been examining.*

Alan escaped that one though, as the charges were dropped when the complainant retracted his statement, presumably out of embarrassment that one man had made him look like that. Whatever, it was a lucky escape…

Billy the Slapper

I worked with Alan for a year in this lovely nightclub called the Snooty Fox in an affluent sleepy town in the stockbroker belt of Cheshire called Congleton. It was great. The customers were easy, just a tad weird. We used to call it Mongleton. But apart from a few big farmers' sons and the odd group of scallies from neighbouring towns trying to get in, it was mostly money for nothing as we had overkill on the door. Five doormen right out the top drawer. There was Alan, Steve, (The Terminator and ex-Para, decorated from the Falkland campaign) a local guy we used as a spotter, me, and Big Billy. The customers there usually only ever needed a good scare to keep them malleable.

I can remember one Christmas Eve, Alan and I were standing along the stairway, him at the top and me halfway down, looking menacing at the queuing customers. We'd always stand there at the start of the night for the intimidation factor. Alan said to me, in a loud voice, *Well, who do ya think, Steve*? *Sorry, Al, what was that*? I said, and he repeated even louder, *Who do ya think*? *Who do I think what, mate*?

He said in a scowling, drawl, *Who do ya think'll be eating their Christmas dinner with no teeth*? The whole queue simultaneously looked floor-wards and strangely enough, we never heard so much as a cough that night. But yeah! Big Billy. Now there was a character! He looked like a seven-foot psychotic Tommy Cooper with hands like a gravedigger's shovel. We were worried that if he ever punched someone, he'd be on a murder charge. So the lads had taught him to bitch-slap. Kind of a mistake as the more he employed the technique, the more accomplished he became. The bitch-slap was invented for Billy. He was born to use it. It was blood chilling just to hear it. I was at the bottom of the stairs at the front door one night with the other lads when we heard him slap someone upstairs and we all heaved, doubled up, and cringed in sympathy for the recipient. Yep, he was put on the planet to slap people. In full flow where he would fully wind up prior to delivery then twist his twenty-eight stone frame towards the victim with his giant hand following in turbo, a millisecond later was a vision to behold.

The first time I'd seen it administered in anger was at the said nightclub. A group of five off-duty doormen had been allowed in and were bounding up the stairs in a very deliberate manner. As they got to the top, they ignored the girl on the till, saying, *We're doormen, we don't fuckin pay*! We were all at the till as it was still early on in the evening except for the local lad who was on the front door. He came up when they became argumentative. Alan said, *OK, lads, that's right, we let doormen in free. Can you show us your door badge and sign in the guest book*? When a doorman is on a night out, even in another town, you show your badge and it's a queue-jump freebie-in passport.

This bell end, who was leading the group, exclaims, *We're signing fuck all, pal*! Alan took the lead and gripped the bloke. We all followed suit, we all had one each and were wrestling them slowly but surely down the long, ridiculously steep stairs. All was going swimmingly until the Terminator got overzealous, slipped with his man, and caused a human avalanche. It was surreal; we were all were tumbling down the stairs, none of us lost grip with our victims though, and as I was backwards, somersaulting with mine, I was totally amazed to see Alan repeatedly kneeing his man as they both were going arse over tit over arse over tit.

We pushed them out the door unceremoniously. They were dishevelled and had no fight left in them except for the mouthy one who was arguing off the step with Billy about the treatment they'd received. I remember Alan saying to me, *Watch this now, Dink*! Alan had worked with Billy far longer than I had and knew him well. I said, *Dink! Dink what*? And right on cue, Billy slapped him. The man didn't fall to the floor; he accelerated there, like from nought to one hundred in a microsecond!

Fuckin' shit! I exclaimed loudly. And then as the man was lying there, completely lifeless, I noticed blood flowing out of his mouth. Lots of the stuff. It had the consistency and look of tomato soup. I turned to Alan and said, *Fuckin' hell*! *He's killed the cunt*! Billy, on hearing me and then noticing the large queue of customers at the door, suddenly jumped back, threw his hands in the air and announces, *OK! Stand back, everyone*, *while I perform first aid on this man*! Like Superman arriving at the scene of a crime. Who the fuck he thought he was kidding God only knows.

Well, that one got well reported and the following night we all took our turn to be summoned over to the local cop shop for questioning. I was the last one to be called. The officer asked me had

I seen the incident. I'd anticipated this and had rehearsed my response; I couldn't wait to give my performance. *Yes*, I replied. *I saw everything, officer. I was only a metre away. Great,* said the cop, *All the others saw nothing.*

Oh shit! I thought, this will have to be good. I said, *The man in question had become hysterical and Mr Harris (Billy) went to lightly slap him across the cheek, to bring him out of hysteria, but the man was so intoxicated that he stumbled to the floor, hitting his head. Oh, right, I see*, said the cop. *That isn't as damning as what the man is making out. Thank you for your help. We'll be in touch.*

Well, I ran back to the club, excited to tell Billy I'd probably got him a not guilty. I got back and told him of my get out of prison story and it seemed to go straight over his head, as he said, *Well, what did ya think of the slap, Steve*? I lost all focus and said excitedly, like a big kid, *Yeah, I've been told about it, I've even fuckin heard it one time, Bill, but that's the first time I've ever seen it and it was totally fuckin awesome, mate*! And I congratulated him with a handshake and a big grin. This was ridiculous, as he could have been looking at a descent prison sentence. Well, I'd like to think it was something to do with my statement as he just got bound over for a year.

Over the coming years, I saw him slap numerous deserving people and never once did I ever see anyone remain conscious. It's a bit like one of them Exocet missiles. You can see the thing coming but there's fuck all you can do about it!

The Terminator

Steve, The Terminator, is another great character. He was a Falklands War hero from Two Para. The army had worked these people into clinical war machines, yet there didn't seem to be much in the way of rehabilitation after the war.

Once Steve put on a black jacket, he was in war mode and all the customers were the *enemy*. He would take up a position in the club and you would see his head moving slowly from side to side, all night with his eyes flashing like a high-speed camera shutter. Fuckin' RoboCop 2! He was amazing, you could be running to a situation knowing he was way behind you, yet when you got there, you'd find him on top of someone throttling them. He was the type of person who would follow you into a revolving door and come out first. You had to be real careful if he was in the middle of a kick-off, though, as there was a good chance you'd cop for one off him.

I'm absolutely convinced the phrase, friendly fire was invented for him. I used to spend the night scanning the customers, checking on Steve, scan the customers, check on Steve. That was my function. If he wasn't at his post, someone would be receiving corporal punishment. I remember one night I looked round, and he was missing. I looked round to Alan with a great emergency and said, *Fuck! Where's Steve*? Alan jokingly closed his eyes, tilting his head back for a few seconds then said, *I can't hear anyone screaming, he must be on the bog.*

I remember this one time a fight had broken out between two lads and as usual, as I got to it, he was already there. He had both lads in a headlock, one in each arm. As I went to assist him, he scowled and swerved them away from me. I shouted to him, *Fuckin hell, Steve! Give us one! It's not like the Wild West, you don't get paid for how many scalps you get*! But those seeds of wisdom fell totally on stony ground…

Richie the Elbow

Another great doorman was a man called Richie Herbert. A brilliant personality, he was Gary's right-hand man. (Just to avoid offending anyone here, I do appreciate Gary had several *right-hand men*, but he was Gary's senior student and he always had him at the thick of things on most of his activities, dark missions, and safaris).

Richie had the friendliest, jokey disposition for a doorman I've ever met. His brother, who was a damn good doorman too, was very much the same. I talk in the past tense here as they've both retired from the game with throat problems – they both choked on the new government SIA (Security Industry Association) red tape and legislation. What a loss!

Richie would joke and laugh his way through the night, even in hairy situations. He was a master at all martial arts techniques and could deploy them in the heat of battle. But his forte was the elbow strike. Every elbow technique there is he was the supremo. I've seen him fire them from the side, as a hook, rising like an uppercut, over the top, coming down, which would connect with all the painful bits down the centre of your face. I even saw him deliver a turning reverse elbow. But the best was when he was fronting the door at the then newly opened two-thousand capacity nightclub in town called Brannigans. A group of bodybuilders, massively infected with chemicals, were posing around the club being sickeningly intimidating with their short-sleeve shirts, the sleeves cut back to an inch off their fuckin' shoulders as they puffed out their chests and sucked in their gear-bellies. They started to become a nuisance and in the end; they were asked to leave. The lads had got them into the foyer where they were waiting for the last of their herd to come through. The biggest of them, who seemed to be in charge, started to get very agitated and twitchy. Richie went over to him, smiled, and started to make light conversation with him. *All right, mate, body builder then, are ya*? The man nodded with a grunt and a deep frown. Richie then said, *I pump a bit of iron, mate too, look*. Richie then raised his left arm, clenched his fist and bent his forearm towards his shoulder in a classic bicep pose then pointed at it with his right hand, then like lightning, with just a few inches of movement, smashed his right elbow across the bloke's jaw. Immediate lights out! Absolute fuckin' poetry!

Goes the old saying – ya can't put muscles on ya jaw…

Richie by no means abused his abilities, though. In fact, he was the complete opposite. A protector of the bullied and only heavy-handed when demanded upon by the bullies. He was one great guy with a big heart, constantly happy and full of mischief.

One night I watched this lunatic who Richie had just put out going totally ballistic, foaming at the mouth like a rabid dog, waving his fists and hurling absolutely disgusting insults. Richie shouted in the most exaggerated camp voice and with a waving hand, *Hey! You bitch! I've got feelings you know, I'm not a piece of wood*! You just had to be there. It was funny as fuck as Richie is a big man and looks as hard as nails. The queuing customers were falling about with laughter as were we. The pissed bloke was totally bemused and stormed off shouting obscenities at the queuing customers.

Another funny one was when he was putting this real shitty customer out. As he got to the front door with him, he noticed the lads had just put an unbelievably angry, small but stocky, Scottish guy out on the side exit. The guy was going ballistic, punching and butting the side door. Richie, still holding his man, got to the front door and shouted in the direction of the Scottish guy, *Oy! Short arse*! Then launched his man into the street and quickly closed the door. It was the funniest sight ever, this Scottish guy chasing the other bloke all over the street with the other guy screaming, *It wasn't me! It wasn't me*!

Then two coppers stopped and joined in the chase. It was fuckin' hilarious! Just like a scene from Benny Hill.

Peter the Magpie

Richie had a younger brother called Peter. My God could this man go. He may not have had the technique of his brother but to quote Gary Spiers – *Richie had a heart; Peter would really do ya in.*

I remember working this big rave with him. There must have been about fifteen of us. The guy who we were working for, a kid called Mark, had a couple of doors in town and that night they were having trouble in one of his clubs, The Plantation. We used to call this place the Bone Yard because of the number of ageing moose that used to frequent the place. Boy, this place was chronic. The later it got into the evening the worse, uglier, and fatter they got. By twelve the road leading to it looked like a scene out of Michael Jackson's 'Thriller' video. Come one o'clock they used to receive deliveries of them on pallets.

Sorry, I digress…

Mark had phoned up his second in command who was doing the rave with us and asked him to send Peter and me up to The Plantation to back-up the other doormen there with the scrotes they were having trouble with. As we were being driven there, I can remember thinking, *I'm glad it's Peter I'm going to battle with.*

So en route, I thought I'd get him battle ready and said, *Look, Peter, we'll be dancing from the off, sounds like all the talking's been done.* He looked at me like I'd just told him his dinner was ready.

We got there, and we bounced in. I saw Mark mid-negotiations with about eighty big lads. I was told later they were farmers out on some farming do. I shouted across, *Are these them, Mark*? To which he nodded. So with much aggression, I grabbed the big one he was talking to and ragged him out, growling obscenities at him till we got to the door where I launched him onto the pavement. As I went to turn around, I got knocked sideways by Peter, who was doing the same to another one. He threw his man on top of mine just as mine was trying to get to his feet. We looked at each other for a second and smiled then went back for the others. It ended up with a pile of them out there that me and Pete did on our own. The other doormen were standing there totally bemused.

The driver picked us up to take us back to the rave, he must have thought we were on something as we laughed like children all the way back.

The best story I heard about Peter was when he was working this one night in a club in a place called Wallasey on the outskirts of Liverpool.

A fight had broken out, and the mêlée rolled out into the street. One of the punters squared up to Peter and came at him to throw a punch. Peter was a dan graded black belt, graded by Gary Spiers, and at that time was in full training. Peter described to me how he quickly pulled his right leg back behind him then fired it out head height right into the side of the bloke's face. The bloke went to the floor like a felled tree, unconscious before he hit the ground. Peter said, *I got back in the club an' shut the door fuckin' sharpish.* He told me that as the night went on, his lower leg started to hurt more and more to the point he finished a bit earlier and went off to the hospital.

He was X-rayed and found to have broken a bone in his leg which resulted in him ending up thigh-deep in a plaster cast. He was absolutely furious.

A couple of days later, he said, *I was hobbling around the shops in town when I thought I saw the very same bloke. I couldn't be sure as he was standing side on to me, so I shouted, Oi you*! *As the guy turned round to face me, I saw that the whole side of his face was in like a kind of scaffolding with bars coming out of his face with connecting pins from the top of his head to the bottom of his jaw. He looked at me with abject horror and tried to shout something to me, but I shouted over him, with a large degree of embarrassment, and said, never mind that, mate, I've got a perfect right to hang my fucking coat on that – look what you've done to my leg.*

I said, *Peter, you never said that*, as I laughed out loud. But it was an absolute old-school classic. Both were injured so no police, no solicitors, no claims lodged. A bloody far cry from today.

But getting back to the *Magpie* bit. Well, I've never known anyone to spot and find money or valuables like Peter.

If there was any money dropped on the floor at the end of the night, it would be him that found it.

I recall one night when he was working at Brannigans he was ejecting a punter when he noticed a gold chain on the floor. So he changed the hold he had on him and wrestled him into a head lock so he could stoop down and grab the chain with his now free hand. Problem was the guy was quite resistant. It was the funniest sight, seeing Peter squeezing this poor fucker's nose and pinching his face to make him drop down with him so he could swoop on the trinket.

On the right, Peter the Magpie

Another time was when I was working at a place opposite him a huge kick-off erupted on the street. Nothing to do with either of our venues. I saw Peter running over to it. I shouted, *Pete, leave it, it's nothing to do with us, leave 'em, they're only hurting themselves*. But he just seemed to disappear right into the middle of it. I got there and

I watched in amazement as Peter the Magpie crawled out of the mêlée between someone's legs with his hands full of swag. It was totally surreal, like something out of a cartoon. As we walked back, me shaking my head, he showed me a bracelet, loose change, and a bottle of perfume. After that night, I've always thought we should reverse the nicknames and call fucking magpies Peter Herberts.

Peter, another great doorman and character alas now not working the doors.

Carlos

Then there was Carlos … I have such affection for this man. He's from the Middle East somewhere and again unique. He has a strong accent and a lot of times he would say things that came out maybe not as he intended, especially with the females. Like when a lady would say hello as she entered the club and he would reply with his pronounced accent but in a very polite manner, *Good evening, madam, how are you tonight*? *You have very nice tits*. God! He was a fuckin' nightmare to work with concerning the ladies, but we all loved this man and boy could he go when it came to show time, and I never saw any woman take offence with him; I think they thought it was part of his culture.

This man is extremely respected in his hometown of Liverpool. He's never not been there for any of us. I've learnt to be careful about telling him of anyone I might dislike or be having a problem with as his instant and immediate reaction always is (in his charming accent) *Who is this, Steve*? *Where do they live*? *What time we meet and is it tools or no tools*?

I learnt a lot about debt collecting from this man. He was very successful in this area. He taught me to treat a gentleman like a cunt and a cunt like a gentleman. It always throws them. Like the time he was visiting this very rich guy. His house was that big the fuckin' drive had street lights. After Carlos had explained the debt, the man got very irate and official, trying to refer him to his solicitors. Carlos replied in his heavy accent, *Listen here, stuck-up cunt, if you don't have the money ready when I call tomorrow, I'll fix it for you to never be able to get a hard-on again for the rest of your life*! The money was all there the following day in crisp new bank notes.

Carlos once said to me after I was thanking him for a favour he'd just done for me, *Steve*, he said in his endearing accent, *It's no problem, thanks is not necessary, I love you like a brother, believe me if you ever needed a kidney, I would give you one of mine*. I think that's the nicest thing I've ever had said to me. I love him to bits.

He is now a very successful businessman who made it from nothing. I'm so very proud of him.

John the Moose Hunter

A man who's worked for us for many years and someone I worked with for just over two years on a two-man door called the Office Bar was my good friend Big John Buxton, a giant of a man.

It was with this man that I faced one of my biggest kick-offs as regard to being out numbered, doorman-times-twat ratio.

We were at the Office Bar one Saturday night when a big guy with an entourage of ten or twelve, all on the large side, walked over to our door. They looked like off-duty doormen. The guy leading the group came over to John and shook his hand. John then realised he knew him. He'd worked with him in a club in North Wales many years ago. They spoke for a while and they went into the bar.

John told me he was a bit of a success story as he left the doors to start up an injury claim firms. At the time he was possibly one of the first in the north-west, certainly in the area. It made him a million.

John said, *It's turned him into a smug bastard though. You often see him strutting about on weekend evenings, accompanied by his little crew of buddies who, probably intentionally, looked more like bodyguards*.

After we let them in, two other groups of four or five, one a few minutes after the other, came in informing us they were part of that guy's party.

Had we not known the bloke we would have knocked them back but as we did and they were all dressed smart and seemed sober, they were welcomed as our guests.

It was about an hour later when we heard a massive disturbance. We ran in and saw it was the group of men all going for it like crazed animals, furniture was being overturned and we could hear glass being smashed.

The place was heaving that night and as we charged our way through, we saw, to our horror, they were attacking the owner and some friends he had with him that evening.

We both just launched ourselves into the affray. We managed to get a grip of the main guy and the one who was trying to strangle the boss.

We had them both in choke holds and dragged them backwards to the door. The unspoken plan was to get them out in a semi-conscious state then dive back in for two more until we got overpowered and probably weighed in. To our great fortune, as we had the ringleader, the rest stopped proceedings and followed us out like a swarm of bees around their queen.

As they spilled out of the door and into the street, we somehow managed to get the door closed behind us with a bit of distance between us.

We had no other alternative but to become large in the door and take up a fighting stance.

The only thing in a doorman's favour in situations like this is, unless the attack is pre-arranged, groups of cunts like them have little or no strategy. They were all individually screaming and shouting and coming at us from directly in front, in ones and twos.

We had the high ground and were holding them off, firing kicks and punches as they ran at us.

Fortunately, the twat leading the group regained full consciousness and staggered up and called a halt to the mayhem, shouting, *Stop! I know this man.* Believe me; those words were music to my ears.

John and the guy spoke for a bit and ended up shaking hands and off they all fucked.

A nice epilogue to this story is that we caught up with the guy a few weeks later. We were informed that he and his brother were drinking in one of our bars downtown one Friday evening.

So, we called in there before starting work to have a nice little word with them both.

We explained and conveyed our displeasure in all means of *communication* on how naughty they'd been and what silly sausages they would be if they ever showed their rosy little faces in town again. Well, something along those lines!

John was the first doorman, if not in the country, then most certainly in the north-west, to get CS gassed. He was working in the resort town of Rhyl on the North Wales coast at a nightclub called Brunel's right on the seafront by the large fairground.

Part way through the night they were asked to remove a group of lads. They hadn't actually caused any serious trouble or hit anyone; they were just being a complete pain with their behaviour.

The lads got them out but as is often the norm, once outside, with a nice safe distance between them and the doormen, they all turned into superheroes.

This one guy that John had launched walked towards the door beckoning to John to come out shouting, *Hey, big man! Get out here! I want a word with you!* As he'd had the bollocks to come forward on his own, leaving the safety of his pack, John walked out to him. *What's your problem, mate*? John asked him, to which he replied, *You're my fuckin' problem*! And then, from his inside pocket he pulled out a canister of CS gas and sprayed John right in his face.

The prick had no idea how to discharge it correctly. He was using it outside and made no allowance for that fact and left too much distance between him and John. So not much landed, just enough to piss John right off. John wiped his face, clenched his fists, let out a roar and ran at him.

The whole group fragmented like shithouse rats, running off in all directions.

But John was fully focussed on his pursuit of the rat who'd sprayed him.

The guy legged it across the road and leapt over the sea wall onto the beach like an Olympic hurdler, with John hot on the chase gaining on him all the time.

There comes a time when you just have to stand and fight, or in the case of a shithouse, do something outrageously cowardly.

This rat elected the latter.

He turned around, saw John gaining on him, altered direction, and ran straight into the sea!

Water past his knees, past his waist, past his chest, and ultimately, he was out of his depth.

John stood at the water's edge catching his breath, he said, *I thought I'd wait and see how long the prick would stay there for.*

John stood there for over twenty minutes, watching the dozy bastard bobbing up and down like a fuckin' cork.

John started to get cold, (fuck only knows what state of hyperthermia our floater was enduring) so he eventually walked back to the club.

John said the whole performance was well worth the ordeal he'd suffered, plus all the sympathetic attention he received off the barmaids over being CS gassed, as he'd played the wounded soldier, was very warming.

I loved working with John as there was, in the main, no chance you'd be going to prison because of his actions. He never had to punch anyone as he was so big, he just used to wrap them up in his huge bear-like arms. The only problem was you had to keep your eye on him when he had someone in his grip. There were many times I used to have to shout, *John, ease up, mate, he's gone fuckin' purple.*

Oh yeah, he had one other serious fault, his taste (or should I say the lack of it) in women. My God! This man had been with some moose. He'd been with the skinniest woman in the world and the fattest. The fattest we christened the Elephant Woman, not just because she was so fuckin' huge, but because she had thick, grey, crinkly skin too. One night, he went back to the skinny one's house, and she'd put all the sexy gear on for him, stockings, suspenders, and basque, even elbow-length velvet gloves. John took some photos of her and showed the lads at the club. With her being so painfully thin, you could see her bones and what with the kit she had on, one of the lads exclaimed, *Fuckin' hell, John! You've shagged Skeletor*!

You couldn't have described her better. We all laughed until we cried, except Carlos, who on seeing the photos, seemed to get annoyed and screamed, *Buxton! You put your dick in this?!*

One time we held a kangaroo court for him as it was alleged he was seen escorting a particularly awesome monster into his car. This hideous woman (well, when I say woman, we weren't actually sure of its gender or even if it was human) was one crime too much.

At this time, I was working at a club come wine bar called The Foregate. When the lads from the other places finished work, they would all call into The Foregate and we'd all have an end of night staff drink together. It was a nice end to the night as we would share stories of any incidents that may have occurred that evening.

This one particular evening a couple of the lads came to me to inform me of a sighting of John and this monster driving off in his car outside this notoriously dodgy nightclub, called The Plantation, famous for the type of female customers it attracted. We used to call it the zoo or the Bone Yard.

So there had been a sighting of John with one such creature at said club and it had been brought to my attention. So our kangaroo court had to be called into session. These were real funny occasions as the unsuspected accused would be brought to justice and a sentence would be passed. Everything would be as it should, we had the dock, a full sworn in jury, a judge, a defence lawyer, (who would be as useful as a chocolate fireguard), court security, (in case they tried to escape custody) and it always fell to me to adopt the role of council for the prosecution, I'd even have on the gown and wig.

John took it all in great spirit. After several key witnesses were called giving damning evidence and four fabricated exhibits, A, B C, and D had been brought to the attention of the jury, he got a guilty. Before sentence was passed, the judge asked him if he had anything to say in his defence and quick as a flash, he replied, *Yes, Your Honour, I'd like 640 other cases to be taken into account…*

I'm extremely happy and relieved to hear that he has settled down with someone nice and the relationship has lasted a significant period of time. I'm assuming the traumatic, harrowing experience of the case shocked him out of his sinful crimes against humanity. This is exactly what British court justice is all about. I rest my case!

The Boxing Kangaroo

We had many kangaroo court sessions, but the most memorable one was called for the local boxing coach, Steve, who worked for us. He was a hugely popular man, and the court case was attracting so much attention from quiet word of mouth that I had to call it for a Sunday evening, commissioning one of our larger bars to close and run that evening as a private function. It was promising to be a tremendous turn-out as people had confirmed their attendance from all over Liverpool, our colleagues from Manchester, our friends and connections from North Wales. So, I decided to put a till on the door and we all paid a £10 entrance fee, which went to one of the lads who'd just been made redundant from his day job.

The guts of the story to this case was that there had been several sightings of Steve with a notorious local moose who we use to all refer to as Jimmy Tarbuck. Mainly because she was his image. A thick greying untendered fringe swept to one side, large teeth with a pronounced gap in the front, a bushy black moustache, overweight, and ageing. Also, like Mr Tarbuck, she must have been a keen golfer as she definitely played around and had been in more fuckin' bunkers than Hitler.

I had several exhibits. One was fabricated at a printers where a photo of the real Jimmy Tarbuck was superimposed onto a picture of a fat naked woman. We then had it blown up to poster size. It looked fuckin' hilarious! A few of us went to the bar earlier in the day to lay out an area court room fashion and take the exhibits, courtroom gowns, and security uniforms. It was the best night ever; we even had it professionally videoed. The place was rammed and the element of surprise and capture of the accused was perfect, with loads of the lads telling me it was the best and funniest night they could remember. Needless to say, he was found guilty as charged, (his sentence couldn't be printed here).

Size of the Fight in the Dog

One of the most violent men I've ever known is my little mate Les. Boy, could this kid motor. He'd trained in many martial arts eventually gaining a place on the British sport kung fu team.

It was very rare he would actually start a fight, but probably because of his size, any bullying cunt would think nothing of picking on him expecting to get the win. But it would always end in tears – theirs!

I tried to put him on the doors but because of his lack of bulk he had to employ his ability and speed to render them powerless before ejecting them. This always ended up with them leaving not in the shape they came in.

Again, there are so many stories of this man, but one that sticks in my mind is when he went on holiday to Benidorm with the lads.

On their first night they were sitting in a balcony bar having a drink or ten. In the bar directly below was a group of Chelsea supporters, one of whom was this huge fucker. Les slotted a load of drinking straws together and lowered it into the guy's pint below. The guy's mates kept the scam going and looked on in silence. The guy was totally bemused when he reached for his pint and found it empty. Everyone burst into fits of laughter when it was explained to him. The bloke tried to force a smile, but it was plain to see he was wounded that the joke was on him. From then on, the two groups hit it off and hung round together for the rest of the week.

One day around the pool one the Chelsea lads asked one of our lads who was our hard man. Our lad said, *Les, mate.* The kid couldn't believe it. *What, him?* he said. *Yes*, replied our lad.

This must all have got back to the big guy who apparently was their champ as a couple of days later he started an argument with Les. He accused Les of nicking his camera. *My fuckin' camera's gone missing, it's a blue one like I fuckin' seen you with earlier.*

Les denied it profusely but to save any ill feeling said, *Look, mate, come up to my room where my camera is and if you think it's yours, you can have it.*

So they went up to the room, Les showed him his camera, and the kid said, *Yeah, that's fuckin' mine you thieving twat.* Then launched a very deliberate punch at him. Les swerved it and fired a combination into the guy's fat face. The bloke fell forward and grabbed Les in a bear hug. Les, being outweighed, jabbed him in his eye with his fore finger, but it went in more than was meant to, right up to his knuckle, in fact, and got wedged there. The kid was squealing like a stuffed pig. One of our lads came rushing in after hearing the screams and saw what had happened.

Oh, fuck, I'll get a doctor, he said and ran out the room like Linford Christie.

Les told me, that as they were waiting for the doctor to arrive, he thought he would experiment and waggle his finger around a bit. He said it felt weird, a bit like warm blancmange. But then it hit him, he thought once the doctor arrives, he'll call the police. So with a sharp jolt, he yanked his finger out. But unfortunately, the kid's eye came out onto his cheek, still connected to veins and sinews. Les got right off. The doctor came and took the kid off in a flashing light ambulance.

Amazingly, the hospital sorted the kid out with only a large swelling around his eye and cheek, but the kid never came out of his room for the rest of the holiday. Yet another one ending in tears at bedtime.

Yes, Les was a great gifted fighter, but as for putting on the doors, well it would be safer having a Rottweiler on steroids!

Me and my mate, Les

The World Champion

Probably, no actually, the most technically talented fighter I've ever worked with was a man by the name of Ricky Nicholson, who at the time was World Heavyweight Champion Kick-boxer. Yes! World fuckin' champion!

I only worked with him a couple of times, at the Congleton Nightclub, but I'd got to know him when he started to use our boxing club to train in.

He was from North Wales and was in the army. At that time, the army didn't have a world champion anything, so when he had a fight coming up, they used to let him train for the best part of the day, except for a short appearance in the local army recruitment centre.

I vividly remember one Sunday morning at the boxing club the coach asking me if I would hold a strike shield for him. They needed someone big to hold it for him so he could fire out some strong kicks. I absolutely leapt at the chance to hold the pads for the current World Champ. It was already going through my mind how I would be bragging about it in the pub that evening.

I made sure we used my strike shield as I think it's the thickest and densest you can buy. You could hold it up to a charging rhino.

He came over to me and politely went to introduce himself. As he said, *Hello, it's Steve isn't it? I'm Ri—* just there I interrupted him, saying, *Hey, mate, I fuckin' well know who you are*. He smiled and asked me to just hold the shield in various positions and he would fire in the appropriate kick. He said, *Don't worry, I won't be hitting it hard as I have fight coming up soon and I don't want any injuries or to knock you around.* I replied, *No, you go as hard as you want, mate.* Me and my big mouth! So I started swapping the shield from side to side as he shot amazingly powerful shin kicks into it. I seemed to be coping fine until I put it in front of me. Expecting him to just front kick it, he didn't. He spun around like a fuckin' top and did a flying reverse kick into it. It took me right off my feet, and I flew horizontally, crashing into a wall! I felt like an elephant had just stood on my stomach. Everyone was laughing as he picked me up and apologised.

I think I retained my dignity as I shuffled out of the gym stooped over like a ninety-year-old man with piles. I got to know him a bit after that, as I used to make a point of being in the gym when I knew he would be there. As I said, we got him some door work at Congleton, but it was a bit too far for him to travel so he left us and got a start in a nightclub in Chester called The Bar Coast; a place where he almost lost everything. The story goes that he was there one evening, off duty as a customer, talking to the lads on the door when a fight broke out with the doormen and a group of out-of-towners. This is typical for Chester. It may seem a nice quaint city, but it attracts a lot of out-of-town groups, especially as we have a racetrack and when the Chester races are on, we have a massive influx of cunts from all over wanting to be big fish in a small pool. However, I digress, the lads managed to get them out and into the street. The problem was, in the mêlée, Ricky ended up outside with them. The doormen had closed the door once they knew all their lads were in, forgetting about Ricky.

He backed off, but the bullying fuckers saw him as an easy sitting target they could vent their sick anger on. They came at him, but to their great surprise he smashed them to bits, sending them flying like skittles. The problem was as he got to the last one, he was on a bit of a roll and he stepped into him, spun and reversed kicked him in the chest sending him flying.

The kid was in a bad way and an ambulance had to be called. On admission to hospital, his rib cage turned to powder.

The kid did survive, but was on a life-support machine for days.

When it went to court, Ricky got a not guilty. It was seen as self-defence, plus the overwhelming numbers against him and the fact it was unprovoked.

The fight Ricky was training up for was for the first K-1 tournament to be held in this country.

The K-1 is a tournament where sixteen of the top fighters in the country from all the standing fighting arts, compete on the same night down to a final, culminating in a winner.

Ricky was still on bail at the time awaiting the case to come up, which obviously affected him mentally as well as his training and ultimately his performance. He was actually tipped to win the tournament.

I went to that fight; it was held in the Aston Villa Stadium in Birmingham where I watched him make the final but lose to the eventual winner, a man called Matt Skelton, who then went on to become British Heavyweight Boxing Champion. Who still had to be assisted out of the ring with a fuckin' big lump on his thigh the size of a football!

Gary – Himself

The Great Gary Spiers! There are hundreds of amazing stories about this incredible man. Everyone who ever knew him has one.

Gary actually wrote a book of his life just before his sad death in 2001. Most of it was written while staying with me at my house. I'm not sure who's in possession of it now and for some unknown reason, it's not been published. But I'm working on the premise that hopefully one day it will be published so I won't go into great detail about him here, so as not to steal any of his thunder.

Gary called us all his family, or The Family. I know he regarded Greenie as his brother and the great Alfie Lewis (whom my respect and salute to reaches the sky) he loved as the son he never had.

Gary was a larger-than-life character who had all who knew him in his spell. Lots of us, even now, find ourselves still using his sayings.

For some reason he called everyone *Dig*, I still to this day, can't work that one out. I would have thought we should be calling him and anyone else from the southern hemisphere that.

His Kiwi accent dictated some words; fuck came out as fack, and cunt as cant, and so on.

We would find ourselves greeting one another with the same phrase he used to everyone, *All right Dig, how the fack are ya*? We still do to this day. He will never die; his spirit will live on forever.

On saying the above, this book would be incomplete without a couple of tales about him. They're well worthy of mention and hopefully, ones that never made his autobiography.

Manners Cost Nothing; Bad Manners Cost Half Ya Face, Dig!

This is a story Richie told me. One Saturday night Gary had turned up at the club towards the end of the evening where Richie was working to pay the wages. He then sat at the bottom of these stairs with a cup of tea reading a martial arts magazine when some guy and his girlfriend came down the stairs where the uncouth twat kicked Gary in the back and said, *Oi! Fatty! Shift your arse!* This bloke was either stupid beyond belief or had some kind of death wish!

Gary stood up, took the girl by the hand, and said politely, *Please come through, my dear,* as he walked her past him. He then spun around like a whirlwind and smashed the guy full in the side of his head.

Richie said he couldn't see what technique he used, but the guy's face just exploded. All we could see was blood and bits of flesh exploding everywhere.

They got the man off to hospital and Gary made his escape.

The following Monday morning, Richie got a call from the manager of the club asking him and any of the other doormen who were there on the night to call into his office as the guy had made a complaint and was coming in with his solicitor.

Richie got together the other doormen and instructed them to play it down as much as possible, saying the man was bound to have a badly bruised and cut face so not to focus on it or make a big thing of it at all. *We'll just pass it off as the usual Saturday night silliness and say we don't know who Gary was. We'll say we've not seen him before; we think he was a gypsy.*

These were all hardened doormen, well used to seeing bad injuries, so this performance should be a piece of cake. Richie and the other lads duly assembled in the office when the door opened and in walks the guy. On seeing him, all the lads including Richie went stiff with shock, and then doubled up in abject horror with cries of, *Fuckin' shit!* Oh my good God! What the fuck?! Richie said they all nearly vomited, the bloke's face looked like a watermelon with a massive slice out of it. The whole of one side of his face had no recognisable features, just this slab of lumpy, raw liver.

We did manage to pass Gary off as some unknown punter, possibly a traveller, and we all gave very bad, differing descriptions.

Gary kept his head down from that club for a good while and luckily, no further actions got brought.

Richie said Gary never did tell them what type of punch or blow he used to cause that much of a horrific injury. When I asked Gary, this was his reply, *Well, Dig, I hit him with a teisho*, (an open-handed palm heal strike) *right on the ball of his cheek bone. I call it the gynaecologist punch, always works a treat on problem cunts*. He actually had a business card made up with the same sentiments:

Gary Spiers Consultant Gynaecologist ... Problematic Cunts A Speciality

Go to Blackpool for a Laugh and Come Home in Stitches

Greenie told me about the time they were working in Blackpool. He said you really earned your money in that town. Any football supporters who had to travel past Blackpool to go to a match would always have it on their agenda to finish their night off there or at least call into the town via going home. This, along with drunken holiday makers, partygoers, and the ever-expected migration of the stag nights, turned the summer season there into animal farm.

This one night, Gary, Greenie, and some of the other lads from the club they'd been working at were having a meal at an Indian restaurant late after finishing work. A group of other doormen were in the restaurant and came over to say hello and to tip Gary off about a nasty little crew on some kind of holiday. They were from north of the border with this one huge guy who was seemingly on a mission to knock a doorman out wherever he went. They seemed to be working their way right down the Blackpool front. Then, as if scripted, in walks the very same crew very much worse for wear. All our lads sat down, quickly finishing their food waiting for them to kick-off proceedings but strangely enough, nothing happened as they seemed to be more interested in the food and extra alcohol. But it gave Gary an opportunity to have a good look at them and the big bald-headed thug who was leading them.

The following night we'd heard they were out again and causing their usual mayhem. We'd also heard they, or at least the big one, had been made aware that there was a big, very capable, Maori doorman in the large nightclub on the front and they were making their way to it like bounty hunters.

They managed to get in unspotted and true to form, the big one swaggers arrogantly over to where Gary was sitting collecting people's tickets to tear in half, passing them the other half back as a receipt of entry.

The guy shoved Gary in the shoulder and said in an aggressive, heavy accent, *Oi, eh you the man?* Gary stood up and replied, *No, mate, in ya go, Dig, have a good night.*

The slob pushed him again, but even harder and repeated, *I fuckin' said, eh yous the man then*, and without warning or provocation, butted Gary full in the head. Gary had a head like granite, as do all Maoris.

Gary wiped his forehead and calmly said in a soft voice, *That wasn't a butt, Dig,* then from nothing to total eruption, gripped the twat with two hands, his lapels and saggy man tits, locked in Gary's vice like grip. He then lifted him up and ran him right across the foyer into the wall, which was a good five or six metres away. As he hit the wall with tremendous momentum and velocity, Gary butted him full in the face a millisecond after his head hit the wall with perfect timing and maximum destruction. As the unconscious thug slowly slid down the wall, Gary continued his statement in true Crocodile Dundee style, *That's a fakin' butt!*

The other doormen rallied around, but the rest of them declined the offer and with great effort carried the unconscious bullying shithouse out.

A sad foot note to this story is: Unfortunately, the prick did regain consciousness and lived.

Surgical Re-Alignment – You're Best Going Private!

Gary used to attract a lot of what he called legend-hungry bounty hunters; I'd witnessed it several times.

This one occasion, he was working at a very tasty bar in town called The Queen's Head. I was on a night off and had gone to the said bar to see Gary over something. It was the start of the night and the other two lads had just got there and we were awaiting Gary's arrival and as it transpired, we weren't the only ones. Just as Gary arrived, the manager came out to ask the lads to remove a group of three men who had been causing a problem for the last hour or so, giving abuse to the bar staff since they'd been in. It looked like something targeted as one of them kept saying, *When's the big fella start*. The manager informed us that this bloke was a giant who could pass as King Kong's big brother. Gary arrived in a seriously bad mood (that was nothing unusual, the man functioned on pure aggression) and on hearing this went right off his swede.

He said, as he strode into the bar like the Incredible Hulk on nasty pills, *You two get the other blokes; I'll deal with the big gobbie one*.

I followed them in as back-up but wished I hadn't as A: I wasn't needed, and B: I would have nicely missed the carnage about to unfold.

The two other doormen, Iranian Dave and Butch, took hold of the other two blokes and ran them to the door. Then I saw Gary grip this big fucker around the neck in a rear naked choke with one arm and took a grip of flesh just under his jaw with the other hand, then with a yank loosened and parted a huge area of flesh from his face off his skull. It was like something from a horror movie. Everyone, customers, bar staff, and me, balked and covered our eyes as we turned our heads as far round as we could. I was told later that one of the customers actually vomited.

The group hurried their casualty off with much urgency having wrapped the guy's face in one of their jackets. We quickly fabricated a not guilty story putting them in a very damming bad light as we awaited the arrival of plod, but amazingly the night just passed, and no one got a tug.

That one played on my mind a bit and I said to Gary the following day, as tactfully as I could, *That was a tad crude, Gaz, last night.* To which he replied, *No, Dig, not at all. It was a carefully executed technique. You know, Stevie, that's the spot where plastic surgeons make their incisions when doing a face lift. You can then lift the whole face off from the skull.*

Yep, that settled my nightmares down nicely.

Violence Doesn't Always Solve Everything (Sometimes a bit of gentlemanly bartering can achieve the desired objective)

Gary had been away for the weekend on a job with some of the lads. On their return as they dropped him off, he noticed his motor bike was missing. He was beside himself with anger and the lad's hearts sank, not for pity for Gary's loss but absolute anguish for the poor fucker who nicked it. Everyone was talking about it, mainly in sympathetic tones for the unfortunate silly bastard who'd had it away. The Casablanca line was now being used with more emotion and purpose than it was in the film, *Of all the fuckin' bikes in the entire world he had to nick that one.* There was an engine part missing that although still rideable, did need to be attended to. That was the start of the investigations. Gary wrote this part down and went to every scrap yard and bike parts place in the area, leaving his number for them to contact him if anyone came in to order that part. The shop or yard owners were all told if he got to find out that they'd sold on that part without informing him they wouldn't have premises to continue to do business in.

Well, that plot bared fruit as a few days later, a guy from one of the scrap yards contacted him with the relevant information. Gary and the boys shot round there, and it was a total result. He had the man's name and even an address. So off to the said address.

Gary knocked on the door and this guy answered. *Are you mister Joe Blogs,* asked Gary? The man replied, nervously on eyeing Gary up and down and noticing the other lads in attendance, *Err, no mate, that's our kid, he's out at the moment*. Gary replied, *No fakin' worries, Dig, you'll do*, and he grabbed him, and they bundled him into one of the vehicles.

They drove off to a farm run by one of the lad's parents where they bound his arms and legs with parcel tape and lowered him into this large water tank with just his head above the water, while a Polaroid photo was taken of him. To add to the whole effect and urgency of it, it was in January right in the middle of a bad cold snap.

So they went back to the house, but still no one at home. So along with the photo, a letter was attached with a phone number, and put through the door. It read: *Mr Joe Blogs, you have my motor bicycle. I have your brother. (Please see accompanying photo) Would you like to negotiate an exchange? There is absolutely no rush. So if you're agreeable please feel free to contact me at your convenience*.

Well, not to go too deep into things here, bike and brothers were very soon re-united, plus a small disruption fee was exchanged.

It always brought a wry smile to Gary's face when that one ever got brought up. He told me, *Sometimes, Dig, a bit of polite negotiation in a business-like fashion can achieve the desired results*.

That bike was his pride and joy until he came off it one afternoon after swerving for a child.

I can remember him limping into my house, cursing as he told me what had happened.

He asked me if I would run him to the hospital to get it checked out. I half-heartedly agreed. I thought it couldn't have been that bad as he'd limped over a mile to my house from where he said it happened.

So we gets to the hospital, and a porter came over and asked if he'd like a wheelchair, to which he replied, *Yes, Dig, that would be nice*. I thought, *Oh, for fuck's sake*, but when he got X-rayed it showed he'd completely snapped both bones in his lower left leg and ended up spending nearly two weeks in the hospital.

My God, that man's pain threshold must have been off the scale. He limped on it for over a mile and never made that much reference to the pain to the degree of the actual injury.

On his release from hospital, we got him back to my house where all was arranged for him. Everything we could think of was at hand, even the phone. But it was hardly needed as there was a constant stream of brownie point baggers fussing round him from morning to bleedin' night.

If they hadn't made the pilgrimage to my bloody house they would call up to where I was working, asking me to be sure I passed on their undying regards and sympathies. Everyone was fussing about him with great concern apart from one notable exception … Greenie.

He used to come apart in uncontrollable fits of giggles every time we met or when someone came up to me to pay their sympathies for him when we were at work. It was so hilarious to see this hard, grizzly bear of a man totally breaking up like a small child. He even started to refer to him as The Leg (if he could manage to get the word out that is).

Obviously, we had to keep this from Gary as we'd all probably get a touch for it.

Having said that, the two of them had a strong bond, Gary always spoke of Greenie with high regard.

He would often tell me, with high praise, of Greenie's serious professional side, being an expert HGV driver and how he used to get commissioned by Harrods to do contract haulage for them, making deliveries abroad where often Gary would accompany him being employed as security, especially if the journey had to cross the Pyrenees where Gary would carry a firearm.

Gary Training with the great Alfie Lewis

Gary told me of one such trip where they were commissioned to transport a white marble-effect grand piano to Lionel Blaire's villa in Spain.

He told me of Greenie's outstanding driving as he had to reverse the articulated lorry something like half a mile up this narrow winding track up to the villa with perfect precision.

I asked Greenie this one night at work. Yes, he said, it was a twat of a road to back up. I said, *Those long-haul jobs must have been very lucrative*, to which he replied, *That one was, lad. I managed to nick his Rolex on the way out.*

A Student of Mine Turned Champion

This person I'm referring to here is my now fiancée, Linda. We met at one of the karate clubs I was running where she enrolled as a beginner.

At the time, she was in the process of separating from her husband. Karate was something that was getting her out of the house if only for a few hours a week.

She eventually got divorced from her husband but continued to train, seeing it as a few hours of sanctuary.

I had, at that time, no interest in her and paid little attention to her, though I did notice a lot of the lads falling over themselves to partner up with her when it came to sparing or any exercise that involved pairing up.

It wasn't until almost a year later when I was going through the same thing, divorce, that she noticed me sitting in the training hall when everyone had left with my head in my hands deep in despair. She came over and consoled me with words of hope and there on after made a point of coming up to me briefly after class to check in on me. I eventually warmed to her kindness and after playing the wounded soldier, she agreed to come out with me. Soon after, we started dating.

At first, our dating was incognito as it was quite soon after my split with my wife, and I didn't want to let her feel any less guilty by possibly thinking this may have been blossoming while we were still together. So when we were out, and I ran into anyone I knew I used to introduce her by saying, *Oh, this is Lin, a student of mine,* which drove her up the wall.

I still say it now to wind her up (and it well does!)

It was around that time I was working the doors with Gary and like all doormen's girls, she soon became unsettled with me out every weekend night in club land while she sat at home. All was not well until out of the blue the perfect solution arose, and I hope this ploy may help and be a possible solution to any doorman reading this who's experiencing the same anguish with their lady.

The manager of one of the clubs we did that was a leisure centre in the day had told us that a stipulation of the council was that we had to have a female on the security team to deal with any female issues that could arise, so the council could be seen to be covering all bases on legal and moral fronts.

Women bouncers or rather *female door supervisors*, excuse me, were at that time a bit of a new concept and as rare as a council house in Curzon Park.

Linda had just passed her black belt in karate and by now had got to know most of the doormen. So, the head doorman of that venue suggested her.

So, there you have it, lads. If they're singing the old, *it's all right for you, out in the high life every weekend probably enjoying yourself while I'm home alone,* get the fucker on the door! They will either last ten minutes admitting, with much symphony, how much of a dangerous, scary job it is you're doing, or they become part of the team.

I do appreciate that the first scenario is the most preferable, but it's the same as dealing with high-ranking gangsters – it's better to have them in the tent pissing out than the other way round.

Lin went on to become a brilliant doorwoman, going on to work for Mick Francis in a huge, two-thousand capacity nightclub in Stockport called Heaven and Hell.

The lads there loved her as, A. she took all the women issues off their toes; B. she was their conscience when they might start to get overzealous with an ejectee, and C. was their agony aunt in matters of the heart. Also, when a bit of physical was called for with an out-of-control female, she was right in there, as a big bullying dyke of a bird found out to her great expense one night when she slyly fired a cheap shot at Lin while being escorted out.

But to other girls in trouble there she would turn into their mother, even accompanying them to hospital on issues like a pill overdose or drink spiking where the girl often needed someone with them.

She would often come home with presents from such girls or their mothers who would call up to thank her. The stuff she used to get at Christmas was a fuckin' joke (no jealousy issues here!)

This one afternoon she phoned me with much excitement to tell me that someone from Manchester City council had contacted her and asked her to attend The Greater Manchester Door Supervisor of the Year Award as she'd only been short listed.

She told me she'd contacted Mick Francis about it, and he was aware of it but said not to expect anything as it was most likely a token gesture; her being one of only a few ladies working in the job.

It was an event instigated by the police and the council there to promote good relations and behaviour between nightclub security staff and customers. Nominees for this title would be put forward after unannounced, undisclosed visits by council members to the venues within and around Greater Manchester and comments they may have received from customers as well as police observations. Then a grand function would be arranged and nominees, their guests, and local dignitaries would attend to hear and celebrate the winner. A bit like the bleedin' Oscars.

She told me of the date so I could accompany her to the function and the pre-clothes shopping expedition. A few hours later, Mick Francis phoned me and started to tell me what I thought was the

same news and I cut him short, telling him between my spasms of jealous vomiting, that Lin had already told me. He replied, *Steve, there's a left hook to this story, mate. Stockport's Mayor has just contacted me to tell me, in confidence, that my doorwoman from Heaven and Hell had won it and to make sure she attends.*

It was actually a great evening, and she was genuinely surprised when they announced her name.

The speaker paid her much praise and presented her with a lovely plaque. And may I say here, through clenched teeth, I fully subscribe and agree she so well deserved it.

Lin and Gary, just look at that huge Maori buff head

Young Dave – A Rising Star That Burnt Too Bright

As I've already mentioned, I used to run a Sunday morning training session for the doormen.

The emphasis was on realism using pads, strike shields, dummy weapons, and various props.

Gary used to check the register and anyone who had not turned up wouldn't get work the following week. This rule didn't apply to Greenie. He would turn up, but only right at the end to follow us down to the pub.

One person who would always be there was a lad called Dave. A big, strong athletic kid in his early twenties who Gary was training up as a kick-boxer.

Gary had me training with him in the week too, and soon we became very good friends.

I used to feel sorry for him as Gary had him in a real severe training regime.

One time, he and Gary went to Thailand to watch the world kick-boxing championships.

On the morning of their departure, as they stood at the front of the hotel, Gary calmly mentioned to him that they would be having separate travelling arrangements. Just then, a battered old pick-up truck chugged up, Gary slung David and his cases in the back, banged the side of the truck and off it rolled.

The truck, unbeknown to Dave, was taking him to a remote Thai boxing camp where he was to live and train for the next month.

On Gary's return, minus David, he told me what he'd arranged for him.

I couldn't believe what I was hearing. *Gary, you're surely joking*, I said. *No, Dig*, he replied with a huge grin. *It's a place where*

I have good connections. They're going to give him special attention. Then he burst into sadistic laughter.

Gary, tell me you're kidding here. No, Dig, I'm not, he laughed, *An' you should have seen the fakin' look on his face as the truck pulled off.*

When Dave eventually did return, he came back a far better all-round boxer. I could see it at the first Sunday session.

We were all now awaiting his first kick-boxing fight to be arranged. That would be a fight that would never take place.

One Sunday after our training, me, Dave, Greenie, and the rest of the lads (sorry and girl) were, as was the norm, at the usual watering hole quenching our burning thirsts. It was the Sunday that fell between Christmas and New Year, 1996.

The turn-out was great. When I got to the pub, I realised why.

A week earlier I'd had my car nicked right outside Walton Prison while I was on a visit. The thing that really pissed me off an' upset me the most was it had, sat in the back window, a fluffy toy gorilla that Lin had got me. She'd made and fitted a karate suit and black belt for it. She'd even woven my name in the belt in Japanese.

So we all piled into the pub, there were loads of us.

One of the lads, Cliff, an ex-student of mine from the old karate club who trained on Sundays with us, had brought his guitar. He was a genius on it, and we had the best time ever. Even the other customers pulled up their chairs as we all sang to golden oldies as he played. I couldn't believe how Dave, although the youngest, was the one out of all of us that knew most of the words.

Halfway through proceedings the music stopped and one of the lads, nominated by the others, got up to make a speech saying some lovely words on how grateful they all were to me for passing on my knowledge and training them throughout the year. Then they produced from God only knows where a fuckin huge giant fluffy gorilla complete with karate suit and presented it to me.

It brought me to the brink of tears … Later that night I did cry, but not with tears of happiness.

At around nine o'clock, Dave told me he had to get off as he was working that evening and needed to get home, showered, changed, and be at the club by ten.

Greenie heard this and asked if he and his young son, Michael, could catch a lift off him as they live not far from each other. He'd brought Michael along that day as it was his eighteenth birthday a few days earlier.

I thought it about right we got Greenie off, I could tell he'd had enough by the way he was playing the table like a piano with his eyes closed as he slurringly sang along.

So we finished the night off late into the evening, me and Lin got a taxi home.

Part way home the taxi came to an abrupt halt, there were lots of flashing lights, it was a police roadblock. The taxi driver explained to us that there had been an accident and we'd been detoured.

Later on that night, in the early hours, we got a phone call to tell us Dave, Greenie, and Michael had been involved in a fatal car crash with only Michael surviving it.

The next time I saw Gary was at work on New Year's Eve. He was totally devastated, as was I. How we got through that night I'll never know; we should never really have worked.

Both funerals had unbelievable turnouts; David's was in his hometown of Ellesmere Port and Greenie's was in his birth town of Southport where Gary had made most of the arrangements. He even had typed hand-out directions to the church in Southport. It was entitled *Greenies Final Rave*

At the church, the vicar made the comment that he never actually met Michael (Greenie) but, *I've heard he was a bit of a wag*. The whole congregation simultaneously gave out an exhaling grunt.

Greenie had the last laugh as at the moment they were taking his coffin out, down the aisle of the church to a balled of one of Michael Jackson's songs that had been arranged to play it out. After only a few lines into the song it tripped into double speed making it sound like he was on helium.

I looked sky-wards and smiled.

As I mentioned, Greenie's sad death devastated Gary. He was never quite the same.

Just over a year later, in February of 2001, one Saturday night I was working at a newly opened wine bar, right next door to where Gary was working, called Edwards. The guy who owned the security company who had the door there was a good friend of Gary's, called Will Evans, whom I to regarded as a friend.

I was doing him a favour as he'd been let down by a doorman who had been booked to work there.

I got to work that evening, exchanged a few pleasantries with Gary, then went next door and took up my position inside.

Early into the evening, I smiled as I saw Gary talking to the lads at our door. They were all falling about with laughter; he was obviously telling them his stories of his many escapades working the doors. The head doorman there, Stokesy, who was keeling back and forth with laughter was motioning me to come out.

I had, by now, heard them all before, so I stayed inside guarding my flock. He then came in and asked me to come outside as Gary wanted to get a photo of us all. I thought, *Fuckin' hell, Gaz. We've had hundreds of photos taken over the years, what's up with ya?*

When I got outside, he took a few photos then asked one of the lads to take one of just me and him. I well couldn't understand that one, as I said, we had had many photos taken as we were very good close friends, so what's the need for more photos?

After the photography session, he went back to his door. He and his partner had been called in to remove some unwanted guests.

I walked over to his door in case any back-up was needed. Their door suddenly flew open and out into the street rolled three nasty looking abusive dick-heads. They regrouped and came at us. The three of us dealt with them comfortably and Gary thanked me, to which I replied, *Don't thank me, Gaz. It's practise, remember. Live targets.*

He smiled wryly and slowly put a thumb up to me.

A few days later, on February seventeenth, 2001, I got the phone call from hell. Colin, a friend of mine who did a lot of organising and chasing around for Gary, phoned me to tell me Gary had passed away hours earlier.

He'd been admitted to hospital in great discomfort. He'd suffered a pancreas malfunction which led to a massive heart attack.

I said, *Colin, this cannot be true. Only three days ago we were bashing cunts on the street together.*

But it was true. Funeral and burial arrangements were being made.

Gary laid in state in a chapel of rest at a location only known to a select few where we had a 24-hour guard on him.

When I arrived, many of the chosen few were there outside.

I entered the chapel, walked over to the open, extra-large coffin. There was a piece of silk cloth covering his face. I slowly removed it.

He didn't look dead; he had the wry, mischievous look on his face that I knew only too well, with one eyebrow slightly higher than the other.

For a brief moment, I truly was waiting for one of his eyes to open and him to say, *Keep quiet, Dig, I'm going for the insurance.*

I grabbed his hand; it was hard and cold like steel. All at once any hopes or thoughts of this being some kind of scam left my soul.

I walked out in a daze, straight to my car without speaking to any of the lads, and just drove around for what seemed like hours not wanting to go home.

Burial arrangements had been made, and it was agreed it only right and fitting for him to be taken home for a Maori burial.

His senior soldiers were to accompany the body on the long flight back to New Zealand where they were met by his Maori blood family at the village and designated site for his grave.

My big regret is not being able to afford the flight and be part of what I found out later was an amazing, spiritual ceremony.

On the lads' return, one of them, a hard bull of a man named Tony Keegan, came straight to see me from the airport to where I was working that evening.

This man is as straight and down-to-earth as they come. A man with massive respect and standing within and around his hometown of Wigan.

I noticed he had a strange look about him as he came up to the club I was working at.

I shook his hand, and he hugged me. I asked him if the funeral all went well to which he replied in a way as if he couldn't wait to tell me. *Steve, it was all such an unbelievable experience.*

We eventually got to the village where we were met by his Maori family and their community only to be told that their culture and tradition dictates that we had to dig the grave. They had the plot and the shovels ready and waiting, and we were told we had to commence right away as his body had arrived there.

We hadn't settled from the marathon flight and trek to the village, we were still in our suits we'd travelled over in, but without hesitation we complied.

When the grave was dug, the Maoris took over giving him a traditional ceremony.

They told us proceedings weren't over. A large spread of food had been brought along with a good supply of alcoholic refreshment.

We all ate our way through the rest of the day, right through into the night.

It was around dawn that I climbed into one of the vehicles there as I was nearly passing out with sleep deprivation and jetlag. I'd just closed my eyes about to sink into a deep sleep when something startled me, and I sat up in a shock. I could see this large figure at the bottom of the hill nearby. I rubbed my very tired eyes and focussed on him. Steve, I swear down to you it was Gary standing there looking back at us all. Then I watched as he made his way up the hill. When he reached the top, he looked back down at us and gave a wave then disappeared over the hill.

I got out the car and walked over to where all the Maoris were and told them what I'd experienced, telling them it must have been a dream or some kind of apparition brought on by severe sleep loss, but on hearing my story they all just instantly got up and started packing up. Then one of them explained to me that that's what they were waiting for. The ceremony wasn't complete until his passing had been witnessed.

Tony is not a bit spiritualistic, religious or air headed, he's one of the most plain talking down-to-earth guys I've met. His story left me in a daze.

CHAPTER THREE

LOC 19

After Gary's untimely death, I decided to continue working for Will at the club come wine bar. It was still near all the lads as Colin (his assistant) had taken over the doors he had in town and continued to run them.

I needed to move away from the dark cloud that was hanging over the team and give myself a chance of getting over my great loss and move on.

At Edwards, I was starting to enjoy my work there. The lads were brilliant, and it attracted a nice young cliental.

Will would call up on Friday nights with the wages and stay for a while and have a laugh chatting shit or ribbing the customers. He was always buzzing and in a top mood.

After a while, his wife started to call up with the money. My God, she had a presence about herself. Her name was Lesley.

She was actually one of the gladiators on the television programme of the same name. Her show name was Storm.

She would turn up in a flashy sports car wearing tight, flashy, revealing clothes. She was in great shape with a shitta' to kill for.

Along with her long flowing chestnut hair, this woman could stop traffic.

What with her glamorous appearances it was passing me by that we hadn't seen Will for quite some time.

As it transpired, he was experiencing some financial business problems that were taking up all his time and starting to get to him mentally.

Around that time, he was on a night out and let himself get drawn into an argument. He lost his usual control and smashed some guy to bits.

It went to court where he got a guilty with the accompanying holiday.

This brought an end to their marriage and somehow or other, Lesley ended up with all his doors.

She had a couple of doors in Chester and the rest were in and around Manchester.

She had the sense to realise she was vulnerable and that it wouldn't be long before predators would get a smell of this and take her business off her.

So, she allied herself with Mick Francis so as to continue doing business under the safety cover of the very highly respected Loc 19 firm.

The first Friday after their merger she brought Mick up with her to introduce him to us.

As they got out of their car, I watched this man walk over to us, I couldn't believe the amount of aura this guy was giving off. It's difficult to put into words but you just knew this man was a somebody, a player, someone right out of the top drawer.

She introduced me to him separately and straightaway we connected.

I did find out later that she'd mentioned to him that although I was new there and not head doorman, I was the bollocks of the operation.

Soon after the head doorman moved on and I was moved up and she was paid off.

Mick always made a point of coming up with the wages, usually with a few of his lads. He liked Chester and coming up here was a nice break from all the high-level gangster dealings he constantly

faced in Manchester.

Me and Mick

We soon became good friends and a lot of times he would come up late and hang around until we'd finished and then we'd go on to a late opening club.

A few times his then business partner, Steve Bryant, would accompany him.

This man was another with massive aura and my God did he look the part. Very amicable and a gentleman, but when he switched it, his look was so fuckin' menacing he could turn milk into yoghurt.

It used to make me smile how the word would echo right around

town when they were both up.

It certainly was starting to raise my status even higher.

Me, Mick Francis, and my son, Judd, who I thought may have had a possible career with the police force – he's always helping them with their fuckin' enquiries

Taxi for the Condemned Man

This one evening I came to work to be greeted by Colin, the kid who was running the doors Gary had.

He was a cracking lad who had had an amazing life. He was a good friend and someone who I enjoyed being in his company. He had yards and yards of arse too, may be as it transpired, too much.

He told me this particular evening he'd arranged a meet with Mick Francis over some potential mutual business.

He never elaborated and as things turned out I sincerely wished he had have.

On that night at work, I was standing in my usual vantage spot halfway up a very wide majestic staircase that came up from the centre of the bar area and elbowed up to follow the back wall as it continued to the floor above where the toilets were situated.

My position was just on where it elbowed halfway up. It gave me the perfect viewpoint of the entire club and I could easily see the lads on the door and could get to them quickly if needed, plus every bird there would have to pass me on the way to the bog!

Part way through the night, I noticed all the lads on the door standing out on the pavement staring at something with what I could see was looks of anguish on their faces.

Then I heard some shouting and one of our lads motioning me to come out.

None of my lads had moved, but I flew down to see why I'd been called.

As I got out, I saw Mick was standing outside the bar next to ours with one hand on Colin's lapel.

He was in a violent rage. He screamed at me to come over.

As I got nearer, I could see something had happened to Colin as he was visibly shaken with a look like an animal caught in headlights. His two doormen there were white as sheets trying to look everywhere but at Mick.

Mick, what's happened? I asked. Mick replied with murder in his eyes, *this twat just told me I'm probably going to be losing my door here to him and is asking how we can facilitate a smooth handover.*

I said, *Mick, there's no way in the world he would have chanced being so discourteous to you and say such a thing.*

But he had. It wasn't meant to come over like that, but it did.

He was actually told by one of the managers of one of the venues he did there that there was a rumour that their brewery may be taking over our bar and as a consequence, the security might fall to him.

He should never have read that much into it.

Well, I thought he knew that in our game big sharks don't get moved on by smaller fish, they fuckin' eat them. God only knows why the fuck he wanted to dive into the pool of a killer whale and try to bite its arse.

After Mick had vented some more bursts of anger, he informed him that he would now have to attend a meeting with him and Steve

Bryant, his business partner, the following day at a location he would give details of the following morning.

As me and Mick walked away, he told me he would tell me where the meet would be and for me to take Colin there. My heart sank. I thought, *Shit, there's going to be an execution and I'm the fuckin' transport.*

Then Mick and the two men he had with him sped off in a cloud of tyre smoke.

Colin then came over and asked if I would come to the meeting with him. He said, *Me and you go back a long way, Steve, and you and Mick seem to be friends so maybe you could play some kind of mediation role.*

I said, *Colin, I'm already booked for the gig, I'm fuckin' delivering you.*

The next morning, I got a phone call off Mick telling me that the meet would be at a motorway service station on the edge of Chester. He and Steve would be passing there around one o'clock.

I phoned Colin to tell him of the arrangements and that I would be picking him up at 12.30.

I arrived at his house and he nervously got into my car. We both looked like bags of shit as neither of us had had any sleep.

We discussed lots of possible scenarios but we both thought that the most likely outcome would be that he would get dragged into a waiting vehicle and taken away to be shot.

We cobbled up a half-arsed plan to get a seat right in the centre of the cafeteria, in full view, and if they went to drag him out, he should grab a tight hold of me and hang on for grim death and hopefully the commotion would become too much for them to continue and also, they wouldn't want me caught in the crossfire.

To say we were nervous was a massive understatement. We really should have brought a clean change of trousers.

We found a nice, highly visible table and nervously awaited their arrival.

Then from the road we saw their car. A big gleaming black Range Rover Vogue. It pulled up right outside the door in a disabled parking space in what seemed like slow motion. *Way too fuckin' close and handy*, I thought.

In they strode, I went to put my hand up, but they'd already spotted us and were walking over.

Very formal introductions were made and then I was sent to the counter to get the coffees and told to give them a few minutes alone with Colin.

As I stood up, I saw the look of total abandonment on Colin's face. So before leaving for the coffees I said, *Look, you may have this all out of proportion, Colin's not usually like how he was last night, he got it all wrong and is desperate to apologise.* To which Steve replied, *No, this man offended my friend and business partner deeply, so corrective measures will now have to take place as a consequence, now go order the coffees, Steve, and come back when we call you.*

I walked off to the counter wondering if the next time I see Colin it would be in a box or fuckin' boxes. I sat at the counter only to be joined by Mick. He said, *We'll leave Steve to shit him up for a bit then get down to business.*

I said, *Business? Oh fuck, Mick, you're not going to drag him away and switch the poor fucker off, are you?* Mick burst out into a fit of laughter.

No, you daft twat. We're going to take his doors off him. He couldn't contain himself with laughter at my comment. *What fuckin' films have you been watching, Steve, we're in the middle of a fuckin' café.*

I said, *We've all heard the stories about you both and I think me and Colin have lost about ten years off our lives last night worrying over it.*

That made him choke on his coffee as he laughed even harder.

I looked over to the table where they were and watched Steve's finger pointing and wagging into Colin's face and Colin's face going from red to purple to white to green.

Mick and I eventually went over to join them and after another meeting was arranged for the handover of business, Mick and Steve got off.

Me and Colin hammered it straight to the nearest pub!

That may have been a good lesson well learnt by Colin, but to me that day I grew up all in one go. I realised how I would need to conduct myself and how I would now want to be known and seen in the main at a much higher level and standing.

Big Mike, me, and Mad Dog on The Foregate

Is There a Doctor in the House? (A Gunsmith, a Priest, or a Funeral Director)

So, there was a handover of business and we now had a dozen or so doors in town which I was put in charge of. I stayed working at Edwards, which underwent a facelift and name change to The Foregate Club.

I loved working there and at the end of the night all the lads from the other doors we had would call in and have a drink with us.

As I said, I loved working there, but it did have its moments and to date it was there I had my, let's say, most eventful night of my career.

I'd turned up for work as usual. Was washed, freshly shaved and polished head, smart pressed black trousers, and a carefully ironed fresh white shirt. It was Lin's birthday, so she was going out with the girls to Brannigans Nightclub where I was to join her after I'd finished at midnight.

Part way through the evening, after doing a patrol of the dance floor, I went outside to check in on the lads on the front door. While chatting I noticed the lads from our bar next door running over the road to the Queens Head, another one of our other newly acquired bars.

I said to our lads, *I'll just walk over and see what's up and I'll radio you if needed.* As I walked over, I saw two big stocky blokes with their backs to me; they had all the doormen lined up against the wall of the pub in total conformity. It was only as I got nearer, I saw to my trouser filling shock, that one of them had a shotgun and was pointing it at them as he shouted deranged obscenities.

I started to creep up behind the gunman. My heart was thumping so much I could see my shirt moving. I saw the lads look at me and quickly look away.

Step by step, I got right up behind the guy. It seemed like an eternity. I quickly threw my arm around his throat and put him in a sleeper, bringing him quickly to the ground.

The lads dived on the other bloke and after several hundred *precautionary* punches, elbows, butts, and kicks we detained them and called the police.

They got charged and eventually got a four- and seven-year holiday.

So, I finished my shift and with one of the lads who I'd been working with went over to join Lin and the girls at Brannigans. I was in no mood for partying, my shirt sleeve was blackened with grime from the dirty greasy unwashed, unshaven neck of our gunman.

I looked round for the girls and eventually found them on the dance floor all half pissed having a great time. So rather than explain the night's frightful events and possibly spoil her night with concern and worry, I told her I'd had a particularly bad night, and I would sit in the lower bar with my mate until they were ready to go. She said, *Yeah, OK. I'll come down and join you in a few minutes for a bit.*

She most certainly did!

I went back to join my mate, Chris, who had got me a well-deserved cold pint of golden lager with a foaming white head, its condensation was running seductively down the outside of the glass. It was more inviting than a twenty-dollar whore. I never got to drink the bleedin' thing!

Just as I went to sit down on my closely guarded, reserved bar stool, I saw Lin whoosh by me like Linford Christie with one of her friends running with her, holding Lin's lower arm trying desperately to keep up as they headed for the lads on the front door, all closely followed by the other girls in their party.

I ran after them and as I got to her one of the doormen who was the first aider took the other girl's hand off Lin's arm and a gush of blood spurted everywhere; her wrist had been slashed.

The first aider was wrapping a compression bandage over the wound and someone had called an ambulance. What had happened was, nearby the girls, a man and woman were having a very heated argument which soon turned into the man (or so-called man) slapping the girl repeatedly around the face. Lin saw this and separated them by getting between them and restraining the man. As is quite often the norm, the female then takes the side of her man. She smashed a glass and slashed Lin's wrist on the arm she had on the man's chest as she was trying to hold him back.

As I was standing by the foyer as Lin was getting her wrist seen to, the doormen asked a couple of the girls if they would go back into the club with them and see if they could spot the couple.

Just as they went into the main dance floor, I noticed a doorman coming my way escorting a guy out. I don't know what it was, maybe a bout of six sense, but an alarm bell rang in my head and I said to one of our girls, *Is this cunt anything to do with it?* Recognising him, she screamed, *Yes, Steve, that's him*. My blood ran cold, and I stood there. Every organ and tissue in my body was knotting up with cravings of murder. I coldly stood there waiting for the doorman to pass me with him. Neither of them could see or read my bad intentions.

Just at the optimum moment, I fired a rising open palm heal strike to the base of his nose, I could feel the bone sink deep into his head then crush. It opened up the whole of his face. I followed that up with a screaming left hook before the doormen dived on me and pinned me to the wall. They picked up the now unconscious guy and sat him down, his upper body and head slumped on the table. They calmed me down by saying that Lin was in a bit of a bad way and I should go to the hospital with her when the ambulance came. Just then, I saw the doormen and the girls coming through with who was obviously the slut who glassed Lin. I couldn't believe it. They were walking her to the foyer to be detained. Their route would pass right by me. I walked up to meet them and asked quietly disguising my raging fury, *Oh, is this the young lady?* They all replied in disgust, *Yeah, this is her, Steve.* I instantaneously fired a sideway rising palm heel at the base of her bulldog like snotty beak which had the desired effect of splitting her ugly face right open like a rancid fanny. Again, the lads all jumped me and pinned me to the wall.

It was surreal. They picked her up and sat her down and slumped her over the same table as her fella. Both were unconscious, both their faces were pouring with blood and sinuses. The table looked like someone had just gutted a fifty-pound fish there.

As I was being restrained (for my own good) a friend of mine, a doorman who ran his own company, and his business partner, ran over to me, they'd seen what I'd just done.

They suggested we didn't wait for the ambulance and that they ran Lin to the hospital and get me off too before the police came. The doorman giving Lin first aid suggested it was a good idea too, as Lin had lost a lot of blood. As we took hold of Lin to leave, John the head doorman there who was a good friend of mine, came striding over calling my name. As he got to me, I cut him short saying, *Look, John, I'm sorry but don't start having a go at me.*

No, Steve, I know all what's gone on. I just thought you might like to know we're detaining the bird, but the bloke has come to and we're putting him out the side door now, mate.

I grabbed his arm and said, *Fuckin' nice one, John.* And I ran outside.

I passed Lin and my two mates as they were walking her to the car and said, *I won't be a second, I'm just seeing someone before we go.*

My friend, Mark, was getting a bit nervous and wanted to get straight off before the police got there because of what had gone on. It was just then I saw the guy staggering out of the ally from the side door.

I ran over to him and shouted, '*Oi you*! He turned around, seen me and said, *Oh no*, to which I replied, *Oh fuckin' yes*.

I threw a six or seven shot combination into his face culminating with the launch of a big power round house shin kick which caught him full on the side of the head. As it landed, I felt and heard something crack in his neck. He went cotton eyed, and he was unconscious before he hit the ground. My friend, Chris, who I was drinking with earlier came running over. He knelt over him, pulled back one of his eyelids. He looked up and said, *Steve, I think you've killed him.*

Mark and his mate, who was with Lin at his car, came running over. He looked at the crumpled body and sighed. *Oh fuckin' hell, no.* He grabbed me and ran me to the car where he opened up the hatchback boot, curled me up in it, and covered me over with a blanket, slammed the boot lid down on me and tore off.

Our first stop was the hospital where he took Lin into A & E. Mark stayed there with her and Martin, his mate, was to take me to a safe house.

We arrived at this house that was all in darkness. Without turning any lights on, he took me through to the back room and said he was going back to the hospital to pick Mark and Lin up. When they'd finished with her, they would drop her off home and then come back here to work on my alibi.

So there I was sitting in some house in pitch-darkness. My life flashing before me. Suddenly my phone rang, it was Chris, the lad I was out with. At last, hopefully some good news, my good old mate was phoning to reassure me that all was OK and maybe the kid I hit had come to and was none the worse for his ordeal.

Steve, he said, I could tell in his tone that all wasn't good. *That bloke you hit* … there was a long pause. I shouted, *Yeah? Yeah?*

Well, he's defiantly dead, mate. You've killed the cunt stone cold dead.

Are you absolutely sure, Chris, I said.

Yep, they've pulled him to the side, and he hasn't moved for over twenty minutes. The guy's dead as a fuckin' dodo. The Monty Python parrot sketch came to mind but without the humour.

Yeah, just the news I wanted to hear. I sat out the rest of the night with no one getting in touch. My thoughts were of my next twenty years behind bars.

It was around 6 a.m. when Mark and Martin came back. They had waited for hours for Lin while she received treatment at the hospital, then they dropped her off at home.

They had brought a taxi driver we knew, and we rehearsed an alibi whereby he confirmed that he picked me up and took me home at a time well before the incident. Once both our stories correlated, the lads took me home.

We got to my street and circled it a few times, checking for hidden police awaiting my return.

When we were happy all was clear, I crept in. I could only make it to the settee where I collapsed on it with sleep deprivation and a bad case of scrambled nerves.

It only seemed like minutes when I was awoken by someone hammering at my door, exactly how the police do. My heart was in my mouth as I walked to answer it, trying to quickly go over my alibi before I got there. It was Lin, and it was early evening. She'd come around to check if I was there. She said I wasn't answering the phone, and she thought I'd been lifted.

I called Mark to see if he'd heard anything and he said yes, he had, he was giving me time to surface before calling. He said he didn't want to speak on the phone and would come up to see me in a few minutes. Those few moments seemed like years, I was desperate to hear his news, expecting the worse, but for once it was good news. Mark explained that the kid regained consciousness. They propped him up against the wall as he was in quite a bad way and the reason they were there so long was that they'd phoned a friend to come out and pick them up to take the guy to hospital. Apparently, they wouldn't call an ambulance in fear that it would take them to the same hospital as we would be at with Lin. So some guy eventually picked them up and took them to a hospital two towns away, at the back end of Liverpool.

What a lucky escape. I still shudder when I recall it and think how easily things could have turned out very differently.

The cherry on the cake was that the kid didn't even press any charges once he'd done a bit of homework and found out who I was.

Yep – Guns, stabbings, bashings, attempted murder, thrown in the boot of a car, stashed in a strange place to crap myself ridged with fear all night, well it certainly knocks the shit out of Elvis's ditty, *Ya ever had one of them days*?

Weighing in at Nineteen and a Half Stone — Iron Tony Tyson

This is my very good, close friend Big Tony Lathom. An awesome figure of a man who could easily be summed up as the white Mike Tyson, visually and technically, as he has the same electrifying effect with his punching.

Like firemen, most doormen end up with nicknames, mine was *Handsome Steve the Nice Doorman* obviously. I christened Tony *The Sand Man* because he puts people to sleep! He had magic fists, they only had to make contact with human flesh and every single time the recipient went bye byes.

One evening of note, he was working with John the Moose Hunter in a bar called the Victoria.

This was situated on the famous Chester Rows. The Rows are a Roman double level of now mostly shops that encircle the inner city, built of sandstone. The fulcrum of this city feature is the Chester Cross where all four major roads, that are now walkways, meet. It's where the town crier shouts his stuff. The Victoria stands elevated on the Cross with sweeping sandstone steps down to street level.

This one particular evening, the lads were on the door outside on Cunt Watch when the bar doors flew open and out ran three lads with the manager hot on their heels. They had been in for some time and before they left they decided to push aside the manager and help themselves to the cigars behind the bar. The first lad out collided into Tony and they both lost their footing as they stumbled down the steps. But even with no proper purchase of footing, Tony fired out a right hook as he was falling backwards, connecting smack flush on the side of the victim's jaw sending him off to bow bows for a good five minutes.

There was an added reaction in this case. The severity of the punch distressed the prick so much that he discharged the entire contents of his bowls. The smell was unmerciful.

I remember starting work one night at The Foregate Club and this complete nutter was causing a nuisance at the door as he'd been refused entry. This knob didn't have both oars in the water to begin with, yet somewhere, someone had served him with alcohol.

Tony was just getting out of his car to start work with us and spotted the fruit cake.

He pulled his jacket down off his shoulders, arched his back sticking his arse out and, with exaggerated bandy legs and knuckles dragging on the floor, he walked over to the brain downer like a deranged Orangutan and with his tongue out the side of his mouth, tapped him on the shoulder and said in a very slurring manner, *All right, mate*. The guy turned around and absolutely shit himself leaping back about twelve foot then started running backwards shouting, *You're fuckin' mad you are, mad*! You could clearly read this bloke's mind as he was making his escape: *Fuck me, this bloke's worse than me*.

Yeah, Tony's a great doorman and a character, one of the very few still working the job. He's one of my best friends and I would work with this man anywhere.

The Mountain and Mohammad

Now we were linked to Mick Francis and part of Loc 19, we were the team in town, the top kids on the block, the real deal. Anyone who was anyone wanted to become part of the firm. We had the best crew ever that was always there for each other, on or off the job. A lot of doors were now coming our way as we only used the best. One particular venue was very tasty as it attracted punters from the two big council estates, and it was a bar adopted by the army lads from the local barracks.

I had to have two of my best lads on that gaff, but they had to be right for the place. Someone who could talk as well as *do it*, someone who could command respect and not bring us too many future problems.

So the two lads I put on here were Big Mike and Little Mike. Big Mike, who is another very good friend of mine, stands just over seven foot with a strong beefy muscular build. He's a giant of a man with the same size heart. Yep, seven feet, you just wouldn't fuck with this man, he might just sneeze and blew you through the fuckin' window. The man I had working with him was a great guy known as Preston Mick. A man who had a good pro boxing career then made the transition to kick-boxing where he went straight to the top winning a British middleweight title. These two worked perfectly together. They were both level-headed and good with the locals, gaining their full respect. But it was brilliant to watch them in action if someone needed dealing with, it used to go something like this:

Preston Mick would walk over first and explain the situation, be it for the victims to calm down or tell them to leave. He was probably the more technically capable fighter but being a middleweight, he didn't look a big threat. So, if they were bullying fuckers it usually provoked the response, *And who's going to make us*? That was Big Mike's cue to step out of the shadows into the arena and say, in his ultra-deep, high volume, menacing voice, *We are*. That almost always induced the response, *Fuck me*! *Yeah, mate, no fuckin' worries. We're gone.*

They had the place boxed off with minimal violence, but when they came up against out-an-out cunts and a bit of physical was needed, boy was it *show time.*

Again, these two lads were, and still are, very close to my heart. They also became inseparable close friends being best man at each other's weddings.

Yeah, we had the best team ever. We even had a lad by the name of Jo-Jo who could lip read. That was funny as fuck when we would challenge groups of troublemakers before they started proceedings, telling them of their private conversation and what would become of their wellbeing if they went through with their leaked, self-exploding plan.

The Badge of Honour; The Honour of Special Friends

The big two-thousand capacity nightclub Brannigans underwent a change of ownership and closed down for a massive refurb.

The new company came with its own contracted door company called Elite Security. They had their own men but knew they would need a very good local head doorman at the helm.

They managed to secure the local boxing coach, Steve. He was the perfect man for the job as he'd worked there before for Gary and he knew just about everyone in town and the neighbouring towns. He had no big ego and knew how to control the lads and keep them out of causing mischief.

A week before opening there was a meeting with him, the rest of the door team, the security management, and the club manager.

Steve took one look at the men they had enlisted and spoke privately to both sets of managers, conveying his deep worries of the standard of doormen he would be working with. He explained they would need a much higher calibre of doorman. Lads who knew and were known by the locals. Lads who looked and were the part, with a richer value of street cred. They asked him if he could put together such a team. *No*, Steve replied, *but I know a man who can.*

So, I gave him some of my best men and it was as near as you'll get to the perfect team. We had big imposing looking lads on the front door to set the seal for the night by giving off a *best not fuck about in here* vibe. A good talker who could work the queue nicely and some exceptionally capable, strong athletic lads working the inside. And as it required a female door woman, the icing on the cake was we transferred Lin there.

The uniform was the Elite's company jackets and ties with their name highly visible. My lads insisted they wore their Loc 19 badges. This was a bone of contention at first with Elite's area manager but when it was seen just how well it kept the wolf away from the door, all became very agreeable. Loc 19 really was the most notorious firm in the north-west.

Every man who worked for us was given a Loc19 badge. Mick had them specially commissioned, and they looked really eye catching, the lads were so proud to wear them. After work, they would transfer them over to whatever they would be wearing. They were an extremely sought-after doorman accessory. Other doormen would push to do one-off relief nights when someone was off, in the hope they would receive one.

Lin and I were on a night out with one of our lads from Brannigans called Gaz and his girlfriend Sarah. Halfway through the night he noticed someone had taken his three-hundred-pound leather jacket. It was a Christmas present off Sarah. This caused a huge argument between them as he was absolutely mortified, not because of the loss of the jacket and its intrinsic and sentimental value, but that his badge was on it. He was running round frantically, trying to find it purely for that reason. The jacket was eventually found in quite strange circumstances. The person who stole it had put it on and must have been making his way out. On route he got into an argument which developed into a fight. The other kid smashed this thief to bits, and he ended up in quite a bad way. Gaz noticed the commotion and the lad being carried into an ambulance. He shot through the crowd like some kind of superhero, leapt into the ambulance and ripped the jacket off the unconscious casualty; the paramedics just looked on in shock. He emerged out of the back of the ambulance to a crowd of people. As he stood on the step of the ambulance, he looked over the crowd to us and held up the jacket victoriously as he pointed to the badge with a massive grin right across his face.

Gaz is a fantastic doorman and a major asset to the Brannigan's team. He has this brilliant ability of spotting trouble just as it was about to start and always seemed to be the first there.

I took to this man straight away and we very soon became very good friends and now we've become business partners in a property venture. He's an absolute diamond with an equally lovely girlfriend, Sarah.

We did go one stage further with the Loc 19 badge. It was a great honour given to me from my self-adopted brother Mick Francis.

I'd decided to have some Polynesian body art done, a cultural tattoo that goes right around your upper thigh and up onto your lower back. I have some of that blood in me off my mother's side, so it was something I always wanted to get done.

One of our lads, who was a Thai boxer, was having some artwork done on his shins and it was him that prompted me into gear. I asked him about the place he was attending, and he gave it a glowing report. I asked him if he would book me a consultation there at his next visit.

He duly booked me in and called me to inform me of my appointment. I thanked him for his trouble, and he replied, *No, thank you, boss. The guy well knows of you, once I told him I was one of your lads, my tats started getting cheaper. I've now actually booked myself in for a whole lot more, boss.*

The next time I spoke to Mick I happened to mention it, and he told me of a thought he'd been mulling over for some time. He wanted us both to have the Loc 19 badge tattooed on the side of our lower leg. He stipulated that only us were to have this done and he would pay for mine and I would pay for his to signify a special gift to each other. I was overwhelmed by the gesture and said I would book us in at the place I was to have my work done when I was at my consultation. I thought I could check the place out before any ink went into skin, especially now Mick was going.

The shop was in the nearby town of New Ferry, that's right by the place the singer Duffy used to live.

As soon as I got there any worries were dispelled. The place was immaculate. Nothing like the back street seedy tattoo shop I'd envisaged; it was more of a studio with a lovely big glass fronted reception. Steve, the guy who ran it, was sound. He was an ex-doorman who had worked in Manchester and obviously heard of our firm. He said he'd heard a lot about me as I was well-known in the area. When I told him I wanted to book me and Mick Francis in to have the firm's badge done, he was over the moon. So, I gave him a copy of the badge and a date was set.

While I was there on my first visit, I noticed he had a few photos of doormen and gangsters he'd worked with or known. He also had a big passion for boxing, so I asked Mick if he had any photos of him and Ricky Hatton together, as Ricky and Mick were good friends.

We both arrived on the day and Mick had this large picture of him and Ricky with their arms around each other and Mick had signed it. Steve was absolutely overwhelmed.

So up the stairs we went to the room of pain. Steve had said to me previously that it would be an ordeal for him to be inflicting pain on me, but to say he would be nervous about doing the same to Mick would be a huge understatement. But the man had a secret weapon. As we each took to the chair, he made sure his receptionist, Sharon, was there to assist him. She was a young attractive thing; her function that day wasn't to fuckin assist anyone; she was his front line of defence. Every time the pain and hurt set in as the needle ripped into our skin she would say, *Oh gosh, are you all right*? to which we would reply, in the deepest possible macho, Barry White voice, *Yeah, babe. Piece of cake.*

I thought then, *you crafty twat.* A few days later when I was having my thigh and back done, when it came to the most painful bit on the back of my thigh, she suddenly appeared. I was face down on a table with my head poking through the head rest hole in it; I had sweat and tears teaming onto the floor below forming into a sorry little salty lake when I heard Sharon's voice say —*Oh my God, Steve, that must be so painful*, to which I replied, trying to sound as tough as possible, *Hello, babe. Oh, has he started*?

Me and my very good mate, Big Spen

We used to work together on The Foregate Bar. At that time, he was European Kick-boxing Champion. He went on to work in London for a few weeks with his day job and while there one of the local lads got him and the lads some work on the side as film extras. Spen does stand out and has very striking features and got spotted and was given a small part in the film. Since then, he has really hit the big time with main parts in some famous films like *Batman*, *Harry Potter,* and *Wolf.*

So, we both had the Loc 19 badge done, and it looked fuckin' awesome. Over and under it we had the words *Strength through unity, Through courage from within*

As we left to go our separate ways home, he reminded me that it was to remain unique to us and instructed Steve not to ever do that tattoo on anyone else. It couldn't have been more than an hour later when I received a phone call off Mick telling me there'd have to be a change of plan as he had a serious queue of his lads wanting the tattoo as a token of their loyalty. So, we relented and a now large number of select people are sporting the same piece.

I owe the door job so much for the way it made me so immensely rich in great friendships. Words cannot begin to explain how grateful and honoured I feel having true and loyal special friends like Mick, Gaz, Alan, Tony, John, Steve, and so on times a thousand. Doormen in my time were much more than colleges to each other, we were a guild, a brotherhood. Every time, without exception, we were there for each other, willing to put our necks on the line inside and outside of work. There is no other profession like it.

Organised Crime, Disorganised Doorman

This one night I was standing in my usual vantage point at The Foregate Club overlooking proceedings when I noticed a disturbance on the dance floor at the back of the club. I leapt down and grabbed a passing glass collector. I squeezed his shoulders hard and shouted at him to get the lads off the door and tell them it's kicked off on the dance floor. I now wished I'd not shouted at him as I did, as apparently the tit froze to the spot and it took a few moments before they got alerted.

What had happened was we had a nasty little group of handbag thieves in. God they were slick and professional as we found out after we watched it on our CCTV. They would wait for a girl to put her handbag down on the dance floor and one would casually walk pass and kick it to the side to where one of them would be sitting. They would then pick it up and right at the same time another accomplice would be walking past, and the bag would be passed to them. This was all done with military precision and perfect timing.

The problem in this case was that the girl's boyfriend had spotted it and a fight ensued.

I went charging in like a bull elephant with a rocket up its arse. As I got into the crowded dance floor, I felt this sickening cold pain in my shin.

By now the cavalry had arrived and we started to get it under control.

With a mass kick-off you can never be sure what has gone on or who is to blame as everyone wants to scream their version of it at you, so your initial response is to separate the warring parties and throw out the crew who look the cunts. Your instincts will tell you who, then after they've got well off, put the other crew out. So, this we did and it transpired that the first lot we put out was the handbag crew, I wondered why they were so compliant to leave and not offered up much resistance.

The following morning, I woke up to see my right lower leg had swollen to twice its normal size with a big squashy lump in the middle of my shin that was bigger than my knee. I went straight to the hospital where they told me I'd sustained a hematoma caused by a strike to the shin.

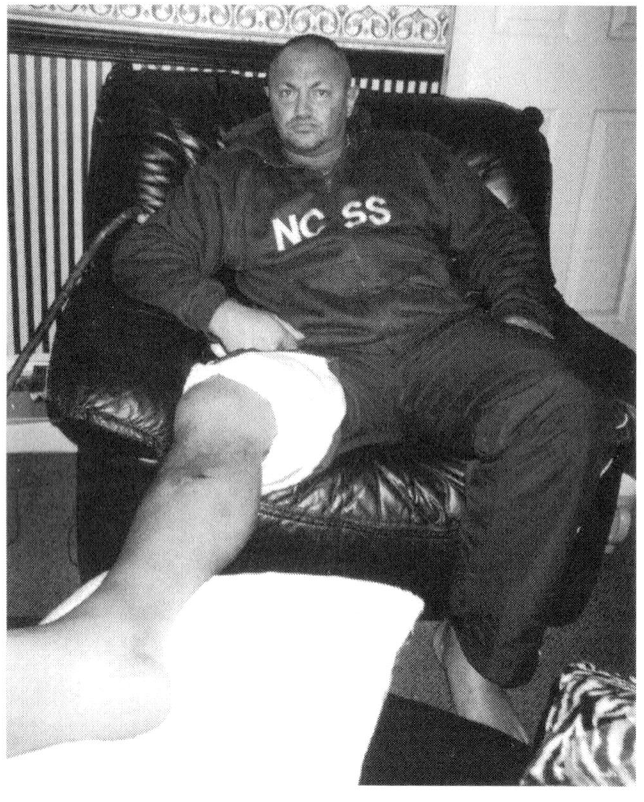

Me after having my leg smashed by the handbag gang

It doesn't look that bad here, but it swelled to twice its usual size and for over a week I was having it drained daily.

God it was painful, especially when I stood up after being seated for any length of time. I had to have it drained every day for over a week with a hypodermic syringe that was the size of a small bike pump. I was off work for weeks.

A couple of days later, the lads came to see me and told me a few people had seen one of them whack me with an extendable cosh.

Yep, they were well organised and with a tasty little contingency arrangement if things did not go quite to plan.

It does annoy me that these days there is a high number of punters out at weekends who carry weapons. The police walk round like fuckin' RoboCop, armed to the back teeth with tonfas, batons, CS gas, and handcuffs, yet us at the sharp end aren't even allowed to use our fists.

Yeah, the law says you may defend yourself when under attack but with us they tend to interpret that law differently.

Like the time at the Brannigans Nightclub there were three doormen and one a female, they got smashed to jam by a large group of shit-bags who'd been to a funeral that day and thought it big to bash everyone they came across. They kicked one of the doormen in the face so hard as he was down on one knee that he needed reconstructive facial surgery. One of the doormen stuck his fist out once and caught one of them, he got arrested and had his door badge suspended for seven months until his case came up. It went to crown court fortunately in front of a jury. Once they saw the CCTV footage it got laughed out of court. The doorman never received any payment for loss of earnings…

The Rave to (Almost) the Grave

Mick Francis phoned me up one morning to ask me if I could put a team of twelve doormen together to do the security for a very high-profile rave at this five-star mansion like hotel right in the heart of Cheshire. He said it was an exclusive gig with only the very rich and famous attending. He told me it would be serious wages and a good long shift as guests would be arriving from mid-afternoon and it was billed to finish at six in the morning. *Brilliant*, I thought, *I'll sort that and will work it myself as head doorman.* God will I ever learn! When something sounds too good to be true it usually always is, and this was no exception to that rule.

I managed to put together my A team and as it transpired it was just as fuckin' well.

We all met up and I was shown around the whole of the venue by the manager who seemed a very presentable business-like gentleman. I then stationed my men on various vantage points keeping four of our more presentable lads for the main entrance. The organiser had four of his own doormen there who he passed on to me to work alongside us. I took one look at them and realised why they'd brought me in.

As I got back to the front door there was a TV camera crew from one of the music channels there to cover the event and get interviews from the celebrities attending the gig. There were quite a few from the soaps, some from *Hollyoaks*, a couple from *Emmerdale*, and I recognised Jason from *Coronation Street*. But the main celebrities started arriving later on in the evening – every bleedin' high-profile gangster in Manchester.

Apparently, the last few times they'd had this gig was at the Lowry Centre in Manchester. No one had bothered to tell me that on each occasion, these gentlemen attended with their entourage in tow. I was then informed by the organiser that on the last gig they tried to ban them which only proved to antagonise them. Each firm just forced their way in past the door staff and the organisers were too scared to call the police. So that's why the venue had been changed. I couldn't believe how stupid the organisers had been. The gig had been so highly advertised and they thought the change of venue would fool them!

As each of these firms came in, they congregated in different parts of the club, none of them mixing with each other. Part way through the evening I was informed that there was tension between two of the groups but before I could get to check it out it kicked off. I blew in a May Day call on the radios and we all raced in; it was absolute mayhem. We eventually got it under control then took stock of our injuries. Most of us were carrying battle scars from it but one of the lads had to be sent to hospital as he had a huge gash that seemed to go right around his head where someone had smashed him with a champagne bottle. We thought things had settled down until we noticed one of the groups had sent a few of their men out to the

... park where they were met by some people in a blacked-out BMW. They seemed to be taking something out of the boot. Just then I got a call from Mick Francis to meet him immediately in the manager's office.

I knocked and was called in. There was Mick, the manager, and the main man from one of the groups that still looked uneasy. It was him who had sent men out to meet with that BMW.

This really grizzly looking man then informs me that one of the doormen during the fight had bitten off part of one of his lad's ear. He wanted me to serve him up so as they could formally execute him in the car park.

I had to think real fuckin' quickly to save a serious situation. *Oh, that dirty twat, yeah, I saw what went on. He's not one of ours so I smashed him to bits around the car park an' fucked him off, mate.* The guy smiled and said, *Nice one, mate. Well, you've just saved someone's life.* I was so relieved he bought it, I felt like bowing as I left the room.

Mick soon after walked past me and out the side of his mouth said, *Fuckin' brilliant.*

Well, the end of the night couldn't have come quicker and for the manager too. All the night's events must have badly got to him as we all noticed his eyes were afire and his jaw was swinging side to side like a hypnotist's watch. He must have snorted a three-foot line. So, we said our goodnights and got the fuck out of there like shit off a shiny shovel.

The ll in Blue Call-Out

We had this great man working for us called Big Burney. He was fucking huge! I loved working with this man as the job was half done as he walked over. His sheer size put most people off continuing with whatever misdemeanour they were committing (though there is always someone who wants to have a go).

Although very good at his job he was a lovely feller. He started taking a lot of time off and then stopped working for us completely, dropping right off our radar. He'd even moved from his house in Liverpool to somewhere in North Wales.

One night, my friend Carlos came to see me at work and told me he'd tracked him down and been round to see him.

Steve, he said, *I have some bad news, Burney's been diagnosed with cancer. They're not sure of the severity as they're awaiting the results of further tests. It's put him out of work and he's living hand to mouth with very little assistance from the social security.*

So straight away I started making plans for a benefit do for him.

I arranged a meeting with the manager of one of our larger venues called Bar 15. This place was perfect for such a gig as it was just at the edge of the main drag of town and the manageress, Tracy, was sound, she was one of us. She did all the organising with the pub side of things.

We decided to have the gig on a Sunday so all the lads could make it. I sent texts out, right throughout our network with the key word being *compulsory*.

Tracy closed the venue and ran it as a private function. She put a girl and till on the door and we charged £10 entry.

Mick Francis brought some signed photos of Ricky Hatton and lots of other boxing memorabilia. We had several raffles and all in all, we raised a good few grand. Burney made the night by actually turning up as guest of honour. I made a light-hearted speech, then Burney got up and said a few words that were very emotional.

The night went off perfect. I got there early to help with arrangements but very soon people started to pour in, the turn-out was fantastic.

As I was talking to someone at the bar, my mate Bob called me to the front door saying Mick had arrived. I said, *Yeah send him in.* Bob said, *Steve, you had best come over.* As I got to the door, I seen this massive black coach parked up with loads of lads piling off it with Mick ushering them in. I greeted them all in with Mick following at the back. I said, *Fuckin' hell, how many are there of ya*? *Seventy-five*, he replied.

Fuck, I thought. The place was pretty much full anyway. But it was a brilliant night and a great success. I felt a bit guilty all the Manchester lads coming up and the night finishing at twelve, so I phoned my friend John who worked as head doorman at a popular nightclub the other end of town called Rosie's. I told him there were loads of us and my friends from Manchester. He said, *That's absolutely fine, Steve. The manager isn't in tonight and we're not that busy.*

Although it was a bit of a walk, we decided to leave the bus tucked up as there was nowhere to park up there. When we got there, we were met by John and he greeted us all in. The night was going swimmingly until one of the locals watched in jealousy his girl chatting up one of our lads. So, he bounds over, picked up one of our champagne bottles and smashed him over the head with it. Our man, even with blood gushing from everywhere, battered this fucker to oblivion. This local kid was there with a few mates and on seeing someone getting the win over their mate, decided the honourable thing would be to all go over and all kick the fuck out of our man. If only they'd stopped to see if he was with anyone – silly sausages.

Yep, as they came over to engage with our man they got surrounded by seventy odd Mancunian Monsters. The doormen came over and we helped them put these shit-bags out.

About half an hour later, John the head doorman came over to me and said the police were in the foyer wanting to talk to me.

I went down was met by what looked like a Chief Constable. He told me they'd been made aware of the disturbance. He also told me he was aware who we were. He'd been around to the house of the venue's manager and dragged him to the club with him. He wasn't a happy bunny, especially with John. Mr Top Cop said their plan was to close the club down and escort us off.

As it was nowhere near closing time, I said, *Look, if you put everyone out it might cause friction with us and the locals as they'll*

CHAPTER FOUR

The Call-Outs

Gary's for the Out-Going Sheriff

If we encountered a serious problem with maybe another firm, a notorious family, or any kind of group, then a shout would be called or what is more commonly known to us is as a *Call-Out*.

It was where you would get word to everyone in your outfit and all your contacts to come out to a given place, always all dressed in black, and pay the offending people a visit, usually at their local pub on their manor. It would most often be just as a show of force with the threat of it being able to be taken further. A good, well-organised call-out would have a massive effect. Large numbers of the right type of men were the key ingredients.

Your standing, the respect you held, and your popularity would all be a factor in the number of men you could accrue.

Also, a call-out could only be called by someone of that calibre as the whole thing could very easily turn into an uncontrollable beast. Men may turn up on a call-out just to be able to take liberties that they wouldn't normally dare do or be able to do.

Gary most certainly qualified as a man who could call, lead, and manage such an event. I'd heard of a few he'd called and been partied to two.

The first one he had that I was involved with was just days after the big two-thousand capacity nightclub I've mentioned, first opened. As I've said earlier, many other door firms had tendered for this prestigious venue, one being the other large door firm in town.

Once it was announced it was Gary who had got the door, we assumed it would push certain people's noses out of joint. The first night of opening to the general public after the VIP night, the guy who ran one of the other large door firms came in with a few of his lads. We saw it as something of a threat, sour grapes and all that. As it eventually turned out, Gary misinterpreted it. Near the end of the evening trouble broke out with these men and our lads ended up putting them out. Although there was a large presence of police, the guy who owned the firm began to shout obscenities and threats to our lads until they got moved on.

We took the threats seriously and a meeting was held where it was agreed this guy and his men had come with the sole intent to cause trouble and show up the door staff and the likelihood was they'd continue to bring trouble to the club. Aiming for us to lose the contract and them stepping in our shoes. So, a shout was called for that Sunday.

A call-out is an amazing spectacle, a phenomenon I believe known as the pyramid effect. The man in charge makes a series of calls to his immediate hierarchy and the message would cascade downwards. It's a bit like kicking a pebble off the top of a mountain and by the time it reaches the bottom it's become an avalanche.

The size of the avalanche is dependent on your standing, how much respect you carry and how popular you are within our world.

A first meeting place would always be arranged for a pre-briefing; in this case it was the Irish Bar where we worked. Gary and I got there early but very soon the avalanche began to roll in.

The turn-out was amazing, I was totally overwhelmed. On a call-out you start with a briefing, mine now are very in-depth. Mainly everyone is told a fictitious story of why we're all there so everyone's singing off the same song sheet if any of us gets a tug from the law.

Gary held the briefing, and the action plan was to visit every one of this man's venues where he had the door. So off we marched. We would go into each place and ask the manager to contact his man in charge of security as we had a serious problem with him and in the meantime, he was to serve us all with drinks and put them on his tab. Obviously, he didn't show and obviously every venue manager was not a happy puppy.

When all venues were completed, we went back to the Irish bar for a de-brief then all went our separate ways.

Gary and I waited there for the inevitable phone call off the guy in question. This came very soon after and a meet was arranged for the following day at one of our venues.

I went with Gary and the other guy turned up with his driver. We all shook hands cordially and sat down. The events that then took place were pre-arranged by Gary, though he kept them quite from me so as I would get the full effect of the show.

Not long after we sat down, in strides Big Richie the head doorman at Brannigans. Richie said he wanted to talk to the guy in private, so they went out the back. After a few moments we could hear Richie shouting then we heard some banging about. After a couple of minutes Richie came out on his own. He had a brief word with Gary then we all got off.

I can only guess what went on out the back with him and Richie but overnight and from that meeting, the guy lost the whole of his empire in one go.

I found out years later that Gary had misinterpreted this kid's actions on that night. He was only there like everyone else, just having a nose at the town's latest new posh nightclub. He never kicked off the trouble. Someone had actually started on one of his lads. He was shouting threats once outside as a way of saving face in front of his men because of how effectively Richie had put him out. It all now seems a tad harsh for the actual crime but in them times, all was fair in love and doors.

Gary's for the British Army

As I mentioned in the preface, the town has a large army barracks. The battalion there at time was due to leave.

Information got back to us that this particular mob had a famous leaving party piece. Just before their departure they would single out a club or bar where they'd had the most trouble at or had been barred from. They would give it a final visit and the doormen would get smashed to bits.

We'd heard that the last town these fuckers left they totally wrecked a wine bar and threw the doormen through its large front picture window.

Information had got back to us that their target venue was our new nightclub, Brannigans.

We held a meeting with the head doorman and a couple of the senior lads from there. From the discussion, we fully agreed we had to take this seriously, and we'd have to call a shout as the place and our lads were now in a very vulnerable position in respect of their numbers and bad intentions. The numbers and bad intentions we could match and exceed. Our major problem was not knowing when they would strike, so therefore, when to call the shout was the issue. But as things worked out, they were lovely enough to furnish us with that information and thereby giving us the tactical advantage. Bless!

It was that Monday evening when a small convoy of two carloads of them drove around the club several times, each time they passed the front door, they shouted as they hung out of the windows waving their fists. *Ya getting it Friday, ya bastards, ya getting it.* They did this on Tuesday and Wednesday too. I can only think their tactics were to scare us and make us more nervous of the impending date and their vain hope would be it would render us soft, easy meat for them on the target day. Stupid fuckers. They obviously hadn't consulted their war tacticians back at camp on this one.

So, the shout was called for Friday. Gary made calls throughout his network and calls were cascading outwards and downwards. You could hear and smell this avalanche rumbling.

Again, the pre-meeting place was the Irish bar. Gary and I had got there early, but almost as soon as we arrived cars and cars and more cars were pulling up. Men were pouring into the bar like a burst dam, and very soon the place reached saturation point. An announcement was made to leave and go to the much bigger bar next door called Wetherspoons. It was quite funny yet very understandable as we all slowly walked in everyone in there immediately got up and walked out. The place looked like the *Mary Celeste*, tables of drinks and food on tables, cigarettes burning in ashtrays, but not a soul in sight.

When we were sure we had all assembled, Gary gave a short pre-brief and on we marched.

On route, we had to pass a bar that was a well-known squaddie haunt, this was a planned manoeuvre, not only because we might just catch the odd squaddie out on an early pass, but also because Gary had issues there. Earlier in the month Gary had fallen out with the manager there over manning levels and subsequently walked off the door. He naturally assumed and rightly expected the rest of the lads would walk with him. They did, except one, a guy called Iranian Dave. He actually stayed and put his own men on with him. I never thought he would turn from Gary in that way. I actually liked this man; he was very uncomplicated and showed much loyalty to us at the time. He had a scary demeanour with his jet-black wiry hair, dark skin, and piercing yellowy white eyes. The manager often complained to Gary that he was scaring the shit out of the customers. He also used to struggle with his command of the English language and word selection which, along with his drooling heavy accent, didn't help matters. In fairness to him, he did try hard to improve his social skills but the more he tried to come over nicer the more he seemed to overcook it.

I remember one evening there the manager came out and asked Gary if he would check out some customers he thought were smoking weed as there was a strong smell of it in their vicinity. Dave said, *Please, Gary, let me check it out for you.* Gary said, *OK, Dave, but remember nice David, nice. Of course, Gary, of course. Trust me.* He was so falling over himself to be nice if we just knew he'd fuck it up, so we crept in behind him like big kids to listen. He went up to the table and took a deep breath before his impending performance. That alone unnerved them all to fuck. He then leant in and with an over rehearsed, over large smile that looked more like something you'd do at a dentist, he said to them, *Folks, please, we've had reports that people can smell cannabis from over here. I'm sure you're not but if you have been please you must stop, now please will you. Thank you please, or I'll have to come back and brutalise you.*

Well, we all totally doubled up in fits of uncontrolled laughter and we never stopped laughing all night. Apart from the manager and the people he spoke to, who were out of there like shit of a shiny shovel.

But I digress. There now was a bit of bad blood between Dave and Gary. So as we slowly approached the bar, Dave and his lads quickly went in shutting the doors firmly and quickly behind them, all we could see was heavily twitching curtains. As we got level with the place, someone broke the eerie silence and shouted, *Av' ya got any squaddies for us to play with*? Then quick as a flash, Big Eddie Lucas shouted, *Av ya got any Iranians for us to play with?* We all broke into loud but deep low laughter as we slowly marched on.

As we got to the club, the usual Friday night door team, and the manager were there to meet us. It was around ten thirty. The manager and the head doorman ushered us through. The club was already quite busy. There was a very large top bar that they'd kept separate for us that was slightly raised and overlooked most of the club. It was quite some sight as the seemingly never-ending procession snaked through the place about five or six deep. The dance floor just opened up like the parting of the Red Sea. As we got to the top bar, Gary and I took a seat where we were immediately joined by the head doorman with news that there was a frenzy of police activity around that quarter of town. We smiled as this was the effect we wanted.

It wasn't long after that one of the on-duty doormen came to inform us that a senior Chief Constable type looking copper with several of his colleges were in the foyer talking with the head doorman. They were inquiring of the group of very large men. They were told that it was just a bit of a lad's night out, but they were having none of it.

Gary instructed the lad to go back and tell the head doorman to tell them the truth(ish), give them the full story and say we are only here as hopefully a deterrent. Also remind them that the manager had informed the police of the threats being made earlier in the week, but they chose not to take it seriously. We did! This message was passed on and the police left with some urgency.

About half an hour had passed before the police returned this time with what looked like a very high-ranking army chappy. The chief copper said to our man that it did appear our concerns were founded. He said he'd spoken with the Colonel and he was going to action his troops to hoover up every squaddie in town and confine them back to barracks if we agreed to keep our lot in here.

That was passed back to us, Gary informed us all and said we should hang around for a bit and have a few more free drinks while they did this then all get off in different directions.

We sat down, and Gary started to laugh. I asked why and he replied, *Well, Dig, I believe I've managed to do something the IRA have been trying to do for years*.

What's that, Gary, I asked.

He replied in his booming Kiwi accent, *Fuck the British Army off, Dig!*

Well, the lot of us broke out into fits of laughter.

Yeah, I suppose maybe in a way he did. Whatever, he'd called one hell of a shout that still gets spoke of today. Sadly, that was to be Gary's swan song.

Match of the Day – Where We All Got a Free Kick

One other call-out of note before I go on to tell of shouts I called (or rather, I should say for legal reasons, ones I may have had a hand in) is one that my good friend Carlos had. He'd taken on a door in a very rough estate in Liverpool. It was a two-man door on quite a notorious pub. On the very first night a fight broke out and the lads ran in to break it up. As they did, it seemed the whole of the pub turned on them. The lads said after, as soon as they got there, they clearly felt their mere presence was resented. The lads came out of it quite badly with both of them being hospitalised overnight.

A meeting was called knowing full well we'd have to

come out over this one. A nice bit of information was passed our way that most of these cunts played football for the pub in the local Sunday league. So, the shout was called for Sunday just after kick-off (start of the match that is!)

Carlos is a man who holds high respect, a man who could call a shout to great response. This case was no exception. The avalanche settled and gathered in the car park just by the pitch. The pre-brief instructions were to march slowly to the pitch. When at the edge we were to split up into two lines and slowly walk around the edge of the pitch until we met. This resulted in us totally encircling them and by about two or three deep. On the given signal and to the count, everyone was to take a large step in at each count. After just a few steps, the game came to an abrupt stop. They all froze to the spot. Once they were all nicely cocooned, all movement stopped and for a moment, there was complete silence. Then the signal to commence proceedings was initiated by Big Jake throwing a machete into the air and then all hell broke loose. It was total carnage, even the away team and the ref got a portion.

Everyone drove off in as many different directions as possible and not one car got a tug.

Some of the lads had said that as they were still driving home, they were listening to reports of it on the local radio station.

I'm so glad I stuck with the martial arts and kick-boxing, that Sunday league football's far too violent.

The Legend Shout

I got a call one Friday afternoon off Mick Francis asking me to meet him in Ellesmere Port as a nightclub owner had asked us to call in for a meeting with view to take over the security there. The club had not long been taken over by this new owner and it had undergone a total refurb and had its name changed to Legends, though the locals had christened it Leg Ends.

We were greeted there by the new owner Ray.

Mick and I got on to this guy straight away; he was a real Arthur Daley type with more faces than Big Ben.

The story was he'd been driving home at the end of the night with the week's takings when he was ambushed and mugged for nine grand.

He was totally convinced it was the work of the head doorman he'd recently taken on. He employed this kid as he was quite a tough nut and he knew and had the respect of the local scallies. At the time, he seemed the ideal choice but now Ray had it firmly fixed in his head that the kid had had him over. This kid was capable of such a stunt, but I believe to this day he had nothing to do with this gig. Ray's plans were to bring in this heavy Manchester crew to take over the security there and get this kid publicly sorted out, all raising his standing in the town.

Mick and I spoke after the meeting. Mick said it all seemed straight forward. We would leave the remaining lads in Legends, replace the head doorman, and deal with this kid that's had him away; piece of cake…

Ray really had the bit between his teeth over this kid, he actually wanted him switched off, and all on the flimsy evidence that he knew the money was being taken from the club that night. It didn't stand up with the police and neither with me, but our first commission was to have him taken out.

Ray told us that the lad owed him a thousand pounds and asked me to ask him for it. Ray knew he wouldn't pay this and that's when he could instigate the hit. This fuckin' turned my stomach. I phoned the kid myself and tried asking him for the money in an attempt to save his skin but he was having none of it saying Ray had got a lot of his things there that he was not releasing that came to well over a thousand pounds. I tried in vain to make him aware of the consequences, but it just wasn't getting through to him. My only hope was to get Alan (The Mallet) to talk to him, I was pinning my hopes on him listening to him. Fortunately, he did listen, and the money was passed to me. I hot footed it to Ray and passed it over, he went white and nearly passed out with shock. I felt like ramming it down his mouth. I got off and phoned Mick to tell him all was now well as I'd got the money off the lad. It was obvious that Ray had been speaking to Mick as Mick's cold reply was, *That's not what you were asked to do*. Mick and I almost fell out over this and I said to him, *Never mind Ray's master plan to get this kid sorted, the kid has paid up and had his nose rubbed in it too, he'll have lost a lot of face over this so if Ray still wants his head, I will resign.*

Ray had to settle for this although he was well unhappy with the situation, but he could now strut around town letting everyone know we were in his corner and he had his two chosen doormen running the day-to-day security who were now on our payroll. They had four lads on at the weekend with them in charge but unbeknown to us, he had those two working off the books in the week and paying them direct.

After a short time, I was receiving some unsavoury stories of bullying there by the door staff, one of these reports came from the mother of my good friend David, the one who died in the car crash. She told me that her other son had gone in there and the two doormen had smashed him up so bad he was unrecognisable; his only crime was being very drunk.

So that Friday night, when I was there paying wages, I asked to see the incident report book. What a fuckin' joke, it read like a copy of the *Beano* with recorded incidents such as: *As we escorted the gentleman out, he accidentally slipped and hit his head repeatedly on the door post.* Or another one was: *As we got the gentleman out, he stumbled and fell heavily to the ground his head accidentally coming into contact with my shoe causing him several deep lacerations.*

The book was full of such lousy cover-up stories. I had to laugh at them at first but then started to get more and angrier, thinking of them bullying and hurting young people like that so dishonourably. It is totally not what we are not about! So I put one of my lads in there as they needed cover for one of their men who was on holiday leave. I told my man just to watch what goes on there and report back to me in a fortnight when he'd finished covering.

The Sunday of his first weekend, he called to see me. *Steve*, he said, *I don't need or want to stay there any longer, I've seen enough. They're battering young lads for hardly any good reason, even locking them in the foyer while they torture them.*

That was it, I'd heard enough. I phoned Mick to discuss how best we should deal with these bullying twats. He said we had to go on a meeting in a couple of days to Wrexham to meet a club owner who looking to change security firms. He said we could call into Legends and deal with them after that on the way home, and he'd speak to Ray and let him know we'd be calling and why. That proved to be a mistake. The following evening, I got picked up and we went off to the meeting in Wrexham. We then went for a meal and headed back home. We came to the junction on the motorway where we should have come off to drop me off home, but we passed it. I quickly mentioned it and Mick reminded me of our second mission of the night. I'd totally forgotten about seeing those twats at Legends as we'd had such a good productive evening and lovely meal, the last thing on my mind was violence.

In the black Range Rover was Mick, me, the driver who was a big lad, and Mick's good friend, Martin Hickman, a well-known bare-knuckle fighter. This man was a real character; he'd had bare-knuckle contests all over the world, his last one being in Cyprus.

He whispered to me as we got nearer to the club, *Has Mick told you, Steve, we're here to weigh these bastards in*. I said, *Well, yeah, I assumed as much*. He said, *Look, Steve, I've had a real shit day today. I've been on the fuckin phone for hours trying to sort out an insurance claim, I'm all pent up and really need to hit some flesh, so would you mind if I just go in and do these fuckers*. I said, *I don't think that's the effect Mick wants to achieve and none of you have met them, so I'll have to go in first to point them out*. He put his head down and seemed to sulk. I couldn't believe this guy, the nearer we got to the place the more my adrenalin and nerves were racing, this fucker was getting a fuckin' hard-on!

We got to the club and all got out the car and headed for the door where Martin pushed past us, burst in, and shouted, *Who's the security here*? And to my surprise, these two lads walked over who I'd never seen before and said, *That would be us, mate. Can we help you*?

Before I could open my mouth, Martin had laid into them quickly followed by Mick and the driver. Eventually they heard my shouts of *That's not them* and they all stopped. As they did, the two unknown doormen made a bolt across the dance floor still screaming,

We're new here, we're new, and made off out of a fire exit at the other end of the club. I didn't know there was an exit there, there may not have been, and they'd created one.

It later transpired that Ray had tipped the doormen off that we were coming, and the shithouses had put stand-ins on.

We all got back into the Range Rover and for a few seconds no one said anything, then we all burst into laughter. We laughed that hard someone told me later the vehicle was rocking from side to side as we drove off…

I found it hard to man this door correctly, men would either leave as the place could get very rough or Ray didn't get on with them and wanted them replaced.

I thought I'd found the right man in a guy who I was introduced to by Carlos. The guy had worked as head doorman at Wigan Pier for a few years, a very large well-known venue.

At the time, he seemed ideal, he even brought his own team. I told him any problems to contact me as it can get quite rough there and I was getting called out there nearly every Friday and Saturday.

This kid was there a couple of weeks and all was going swimmingly, he seemed to be keeping a lid on things nicely. Until, that is, one night, he called up to see me. He informed me that he was experiencing a lot of trouble from lads off the nearby estate. He'd been told the manager from the pub on that estate was instigating it, he thought it was something to do with the guy losing trade to our place.

I bought into this story too quickly without checking it out, a thing I never do these days, whatever the problem that's brought me that I may have to deal with I've found over the years that most often there's a whole other differing side to the story.

But my immediate reply to him was, *OK, mate, lets pay them a little visit.*

I got straight to work calling and texting, informing all our men and all my contacts that there was a shout on. The pre-meeting place was the club as it was only a short walk away to the offending pub. I'd arranged it for Sunday. Unless the situation dictates otherwise, Sunday is the favoured day for call-outs, you'll get a bigger turn-out as most people aren't working that night and also, Sunday is a popular night out for punters so the shout will have the desired effect at the place you're visiting.

I got to the club early with a few of our men. I was quite nervous as this was the first shout I'd ever called. I was worried I wouldn't get sufficient numbers. My worries were unfounded as more and more men arrived at the place. I never involved Mick and the Manchester lads as I thought it was a bit trivial for their involvement and as things turned out I was right. But nevertheless, it was a healthy turn-out with respectable numbers, probably around fifty of us.

But the absolute cherry on the cake was just as I was about to give the pre-brief, I got a tap on my shoulder with a voice saying, *How are ya, Dig*? It was someone imitating Gary's famous greeting but with a heavy Liverpool accent. I turned around to see to my amazement and honour it was Alfie Lewis. He was at that time and probably still is the biggest name and most respected man in Liverpool. He is very well-known in the martial arts word being a five times world champion free style fighter.

I'd met him several times with Gary and got to know him that way. We are now, and I'm absolutely honoured to say, good friends. I think, after Gary died, he kept an eye on me as maybe a parting sentiment to Gary. He said, *You might not see much of me, Steve, but I do keep my eye on you from over the water, I heard you were looking into something, so I thought I'd pop up and check-up in person.*

I gave the pre-brief and we marched over, through the estate, and on into the pub. It was quite busy and as we all filed into the bar you could see the look of shock on people's faces. The landlord came rushing over and me, him, and my head doorman sat down at a table as I told him the reason for our visit and what future consequences there would be if troubles continued.

He listened in shock and total bemusement. He then explained that he hadn't been there that long as the place had a high turnover of managers. He informed me that he had no influence on the local lads whatsoever and that it was just a very hard, rough area, he said they probably had more fights in there. He pleaded with me to believe him and said the last thing he wanted was to piss us off. He explained that the main players on the estate had a lot of respect for me and my firm; it's just that the young lads do get feisty and let off steam like that.

He was right about people of that estate and in the town in general, it's a town that's been built around the port there and like a lot of other port yard towns it has a higher-than-average, hard tough men ratio, but along with that they have big hearts. I've since made some of my best friends from that town.

I got up and shook his hand and said if there was anything we could do together concerning persistent troublemakers he shouldn't hesitate to get in touch with me. With that, I dragged my men back to the club.

That one may have been a mistake or an overreaction, but it certainly raised my standing. The word had got around like wildfire about the shout and the high level of senior heads who attended it. My friend Alan phoned me up only minutes after we got back asking, *What the fuck was all that about, Steve? Alfie Lewis on the Westminster estate!* Yeah, it was a sledgehammer to crack a nut that didn't require cracking but as I said, it was the start of my rise to notoriety.

The Ponderosa Shout

It was getting near to Christmas, yeah, the season of *good will to all men* (for fuck's sake). In Chester at that time, we were experiencing more than usual violent incidents. It was of great concern to me as things could only escalate and like I said, the silly season was almost upon us.

One particular night, two coppers were trying to arrest a giant of a man near to one of our venues. The man was a well-known hard knock from Blacon, the local big estate, though we knew it as the Ponderosa. He was giving the coppers unmerciful problems throwing them around like rag dolls. One of my men, Big Tony, who was working nearby went over to assist them, as I tell all our lads to do if the police are having problems, it might just be a *get out of prison card* one day. Anyway, Tony went over and put this thug straight into a sleeper. He fell to the floor in seconds and the two, much unprepared police officers cuffed him up and called for the meat wagon. The police then said to Tony, *Where the fuck did you learn that?* Tony told them of the training courses I put on. He told them, *Our boss does these courses for our lads and a lot of lads from other companies called Minimum Injury Ejection Techniques.* After a while the officers returned with another cop and asked of the possibility of them attending one of my seminars in a civilian capacity. Tony passed that one on to me, but I thought it best to decline.

That following week we were getting reports that the natives from that estate were voicing their displeasure over the kid getting arrested and Tony's part in it, then alarmingly we then got information of a meeting that had taken place where they were making plans to come up and stab Tony.

This was the ignition to go into motion as I felt like we needed to make some kind of statement there with the troubles we'd been experiencing but this now had taken it up to an urgent level.

I take all threats to our doormen very seriously but this one really worried me. I got my senior men together to discuss how best to deal with the situation and it was agreed we needed to deal with this heavily and immediately, so a shout was called. This time I left no one out, all our doormen, every doorman I knew, every friend and every contact all got contacted.

The initial response I was getting was encouraging. Well *encouraging* wasn't the word. If I knew then of the response I was to get, I think I would have shit it right up to the target day.

As I did have a bit of an idea of the response, I knew I would have to plan it out very thoroughly. We were to target the two pubs on the estate so as usual, I'd planned a pre-briefing place, it was a big eating house type pub on the edge of the estate but as I had a slight inkling of the size of the impending avalanche, I'd planned several other venues for different groups to meet up at before all meeting up at the main pre-briefing pub. This was to not give anyone time to report us; if we all just met at the one place it would spook everyone in a ten-mile radius as the place was slowly filling up with very large gruesome looking men. This way we'd all get to the place pretty much together and there upon we would only have to spend a short period of time there.

Well, that was the plan! I met my men in an out-of-the-way pub just on the outskirts of town, I was just waiting for word off all the other pre-planned meeting places that all had assembled and was good to go. After a while all had blown in confirming they were ready and set to go, I was just now waiting for the Manchester lads. I then received a call off Mick telling me they were caught up in a solid traffic jam on the motorway. After the shout I'd arranged for us to all spend the evening in one of our nightclubs as something of a night out, another excuse for us all being together, so I told them to go straight to the club and we'd meet up with them later.

So, I gave the word to all the other places to move on to the pre-briefing pub. The adrenalin in me was starting to pump as it was then when I gave the order to my lads to move on that I noticed just how many men were in my place, there was doubly enough numbers to pull this one off from there alone.

So, we drove off to the pub for the pre-brief. It was, as I've said, a very large food type pub just on the edge of the estate. As we got there, some of the other groups had arrived. I went in and nearly passed out. The place was heaving with obvious looking large gentlemen all in black. I had to get them all to assemble in the car park as there was two or three other groups yet to get there that would have brought the place to saturation point. Then, as the final group arrived, I gave the pre-briefing in the car park as quickly as I could.

A pre-briefing is so we all have the same story for why we're assembled. I'll always first ask if someone has or soon got a birthday. I read somewhere that if you have at least twenty people together, someone will have a birthday in that week. As you can imagine, several people put their hands up, but one lad was actually forty that day. I also always make sure we have someone from the targeted area, so that then was the story. I announced, *Right, lads, here's the script – we're all here for Steven Short's fortieth birthday. Mr Francis Parker (the local kid from that estate) is hosting the first part of the evening at his pub here in Blacon, so, lads, remember the story if you get a tug, remember those two names otherwise this becomes an illegal gathering. So, lads, get in your vehicles and wait for my signal to roll, please try to stay in convoy.*

How a call-out convoy works is you have your local man in the lead vehicle to guide you to the targeted venue. I'll always be in the second car and I'll have my next in command at the rear. I'll remain in constant communication with these two vehicles. When you get to the targeted venue you don't get out of your vehicle until the rear vehicle confirms his arrival. Your rear man has to be someone switched on as it's he and you that controls and holds the convoy together if it gets temporarily split up, like getting caught at traffic lights etc.

My heart was beating a thousand to the minute. This was the biggest call-out I'd ever been involved with or had ever even heard of.

The first of the pubs we were to visit was about a mile away. As we got there, I again blew into my man at the rear, and he informed me that it was only just then that the last of the cars were leaving the car park there and he'd only just started off. What an incredible sight, all I could see in the car mirror was an endless stream of car lights.

When my man in the rear vehicle had checked in, I gave the order and we all got out of our cars, the noise of car doors slamming was deafening. We all went to walk in when a guy came out of the pub. He was absolutely paralytic, he took one look at all of us and shit himself. He ran to his car that was alongside mine by the pub. He was in shear panic; he eventually managed to get his key in the door and accelerated off. We all watched as he swerved and over revved it, completely losing control, eventually knocking into my fuckin' car. He got out and ran straight back into the pub. We all looked on in stunned amazement. Right at that moment, I got a call off the Manchester lads saying they were now in town. I told them to just wait for us at the club, but they were having none of it saying they hadn't come all the way down here to then miss out on the gig. So, I gave them directions to the pre-briefing pub and I then had to give the order for us all to return back to the pub we had just left to wait for our Manchester colleges.

Now I was really nervous. As we were driving back, I saw people in the streets or at their gates then running into their houses, the police station's phones must have been on complete melt down.

As we got back, the Manchester lads were already there. I again gave the re-briefing only this time we were going to give that last pub a miss as there had been too much activity there, so the plan and destination was set for just the other pub. It was the main one there anyway and that being the reason why we were leaving it to last.

As I was giving the brief, I was scanning my head from side to side viewing the vast sea of men assembled. As I got in the car, my driver told me he'd counted the cars on his doorman's number clicker, he informed me it read one hundred and forty-eight. I said, *You've got to be fuckin' joking, a hundred and forty-eight*? *Yeah*, he replied, *and that's just the cars, no one's turned up on their own, a lot of the cars are full.*

So, wagons roll once more.

An after party following one of the call-outs. We really needed a wider-angle lens as the picture didn't capture all of us. Notice we're all in black but Mick threw on a white coat for the picture!

Same detail as last time, local kid in front, me in vehicle number two and my man on rear guard. We arrive at the target pub and once the last car man blew in, we all got out and headed for the pub. The pub was a fairly large one and normally quite busy but this night as we walked in the place was almost empty apart from the bar staff and a

couple of middle-aged drunks at the bar. I'd found out later that word had got out after we had visited the first place and people had been diving through windows to escape before we got here.

If your call-out is the show of force type it doesn't matter if there's not many people at the place you're targeting, it can actually work in your favour as Chinese whispers go out and what in reality is a fifty-man shout, ends up as hundred men. Also, there's less chance of it turning physical. All in all, if the offending persons are not there it can be better, you get your point over and no one gets a tug.

We all filed into the place and the manageress was desperately flitting round trying to talk to us.

We stayed for only a few minutes and I gave the word to move out. As we were leaving, one of the drunks at the bar started shouting racial abuse at us as we had a lot of black and Asian lads with us. The manageress ran over and put her hand over his foul mouth. A couple of lads went over and gave the prick a slap. This could have turned bad if it wasn't for the brave actions of the manageress who got herself between us and him and screamed apologies on his behalf.

Well, mission accomplished and pretty much violence free. Job done.

We all made our way back to town. First to one of our bars where there was a karaoke on. I'd planned for us to go there as we had a lad who had this great party piece. He would get them to put on the Shania Twain's 'Man, I Feel Like A Woman', but he has his own words to it, his version's called 'Man, It's Great Being A Doorman'. Believe me, it's the funniest thing ever, plus he does all the actions. He had everyone in absolute stitches. It's so funny that the next time he performs it, we're going to video him and send it to a TV producer.

Duvain, singing his version of Shania Twain's 'Man, I Feel Like a Women' called 'Man, It's Great Being a Doorman'.

After him, a whole stream of lads got up, I couldn't believe the talent we had there. One kid sang the Roy Orbison song 'Pretty Woman' so well it seemed like he was miming to the actual record. Then my mate Preston Mick got up and did Elvis's 'In the Ghetto' to stunned silence. You'd have thought Elvis was in the building. We then went over to the nightclub to finish off the evening.

We all had a great night; we well achieved our objective, and no one got a tug.

The following day, questions were being asked but all in all it was a safe, well-planned, well-controlled affective piece of PR. The proof of the pudding being we had a nice low violent Christmas period and Big Tony still with us.

That, to date, was the biggest shout I've ever called, been on, or ever heard of. It was the most amazing sight I think I've ever witnessed. I know you can have larger crowds of football supporters or other types of gathering but these were all hard, tough, large fighting men and we had a lot of serious high-ranking faces there, more than I've ever seen gathered in one place before. We actually had two famous, very well-known ex-world champion kick-boxers there, one being Russ Williams who's now the most respected trainer in Wales and who's recently had a TV documentary made of him; and the other was the two times word champion, Eugene Valerio.

And what with the very high-ranking Manchester and Liverpool heads who turned up too it elevated it into a complete one off. We still have the odd bits of shit, but nothing that could be construed as organised as that shout has gone down in folk law. Anyone who has designs on taking my sheriff's badge off me has this to contemplate - Do you want that coming through your fuckin' door?

It was a privilege and honour to be part of such an epic event. It will remain a memory which I'll carry to my grave.

Me with three Old Lion Word Champions; Left to right – Eugene

Valerio, Terry O'Neill, me, and Russ Williams.

The Warrington Farce

We had a lad who worked for us who was a real *in your face* type of character. At first, I took him as a friend as he'd been introduced to me via a couple of my senior men.

I first put him on at the Legends nightclub but soon had to remove him as he was pissing off the locals there. I should have smelt a rat then, but I chose to believe his side of things and I moved him to Chester to a nice city-centre bar. He eventually left on his own accord but still kept close links with us, always turning up on our nights out or invited himself to any other of our gigs. After he'd left our employment, I found out he would often turn up for work late and on several occasions, he would be incorrectly dressed and worst of all, would drink on duty. The other lads didn't want to grass him up to me, but I believe it was them that encouraged him to resign.

Celebrations after a successful shout – would you buy a second-hand car off any of these gentlemen?

On the night of the Ponderosa shout, he turned up. I was surprised as I'd not contacted him. He gave me some bullshit about his undying loyalty to me and always being there for us. Again, I should have seen through him.

Straight after the shout he came to me telling me he was being terrorised in his hometown of Warrington by some nasty bullying family and could I look into it by maybe bringing some lads up one night to speak to them. He then reminded me how he was always there for us.

After he'd left me, a couple of lads came to tell me of how he'd been contacting them asking them to come up to his local to back him up against these people. On each request the lads kept telling him, yeah fine but run it by the boss. I couldn't believe he was going behind my back like that. So, after hitting several brick walls he came to me and I agreed to look into it.

I took all the details off him and contacted my man Paul in Warrington. This kid, Pagey, as he was better known as, was the well-known hard man of that town and one brilliant doorman. He worked for us at the Legends nightclub as head doorman for over a year and in that time not once did I have to attend to any problems there.

I told him all the details which were met with laughter. He knew my man and regarded him as an unreliable. He also knew the family he was running up against and told me they were nobodies, he told me my missus could do em in. I laughed with him but nevertheless said to him that even though it's a bit trivial we'd have to pop up there if only to stop him pestering the lads.

So, a shout was called, and the first meeting place was one of our venues in Chester. After I gave the pre-briefing, we set off with the Warrington kid in the lead car, big mistake! That night we were actually doing a double as there was a bit of business needed attending to in town so while we had everyone together, I thought we could take the opportunity to tidy that one up too. Again, big mistake!

So, we set off to Warrington with mastermind in lead vehicle. His driving was unbelievable. He was speeding through lights, not properly indicating, and he broke communications with me thus splitting up the convoy.

I was shouting and flashing my headlights but to no avail.

As we got to the target venue, only about half the convoy were in attendance. We were all standing outside the place as I was taking phone calls off lads who'd got lost. My instructions to them were to find the well-known nightclub there called Mr Smith's that you come to just as you get into the town. I told them to wait in the car park and we'd pick them up on the way out.

As I was on the phone, police cars were driving around, and I assumed we'd already been spotted. One of the lads informed me that there was a little crew in the pub, and they were all busy on their mobiles … presumably contacting their mates. So, we now had to act quickly. I got us all together and we entered the pub. Most of the punters who had been in there had now made their exit. I went up to the bar and pulled the very startled barman and told him to pass on a message to the offending lads who we knew used that pub. This he keenly agreed to do, his head was still nodding as we left.

So now we had to hot foot it out of town but first we needed to fly by Mr Smith's to pick up the others. My rear car man that day was my mate John, he was there at Smith's with the rest of the lost group. I instructed him to take up the lead position of that group and as we drove past, to fall in line behind us. What I hadn't realised was his driver was this tosser who hadn't been with us long. As it transpired this kid was whiter than fuckin' white, fuck only knows what possessed him to become a doorman or how he managed to get in with us. As we got up to Smith's car park, I halted the cars behind me, and I swung round into the car park. I shouted to John to fall in behind the last car and when all were in procession, to drop back and take up the rear position, then to blow in to confirm.

I swerved in and out of the car park still angry and drove off to the motorway onto our next mission.

After about ten minutes I realised I'd not heard from John. I phoned him to check all was well. *John, all OK, mate?* I asked. *Well, no, boss*, he nervously replied, *we've kinda all got lost. What*? I screamed, deafening everyone in the car. *Where the pissin' fuckin' bastarding hell are you*? I was so angry I was actually foaming at the mouth.

Steve, I'm sorry, mate, it's Paul the driver, he said you made an illegal manoeuvre as you came out of the car park.

What the pissin' fuckin' hell are you fuckin' on about, John?

Well, sorry, boss. He said you crossed a double white line when you came out, so he turned left to find a roundabout and everyone behind us followed and now we're all lost, boss.

That was the final straw, I just totally lost it. I was screaming down the phone as I was butting and punching the steering wheel. With that, I must have dislodged something as then the horn came on. It seemed louder than normal. Oh, fuckin' great that's all we need. We're meant to be off on a mission under the cover of fuckin' darkness and I've got my horn blowing off like a fuckin' air-raid siren. Then I started to punch the roof of the car as I cursed this Paul guy to hell and back.

We were on the motorway at this point, so I pulled over onto the hard shoulder to disconnect the horn. As I stopped, the other three men with me shot out of the car and ran up the grass bank. The other cars pulled up alongside of me and asked what was happening. The lads up on the grass bank shouted, *Someone will have to give us a lift, we're not getting back in there with him, he's lost it, he's gone fuckin' mad.*

Well, we fixed the horn and all eventually all hooked up.

We completed the other business, then hit the pub where we then saw the funny side of it all, well they did as the three that were in my car were doing impressions of Steve the alien from The Planet Super Strop to a bit too appreciative an audience.

That Warrington kid did eventually prove to be an unloyal dishonourable traitor. After that call-out, I personally sorted two other bad problems out for him only for him then to turn on me and Mick.

Well in my book, he's the loser as I believe everything is meaningless without friendship.

The Shout for the Old People Bashers

One of the lads came to see me to ask for my opinion on what was a horrible issue. He said he was hesitant to see me on this matter as it was of a family nature and nothing to do with work. I told him that's what makes us different, we're always there for one another be it work or personal. The story was his elderly mother was living in a small block of flats which had been set aside for OAPs.

Somehow or other, one of the flats had been sub-let to three young scrotes, nasty horrible lads in their early twenties. His mother had told him they were playing their music at full belt right through the night. All the residents there were scared of them and never complained. Unfortunately, my man's mother, even at a ripe old age, had a bit of grit about her and one night in the early hours she knocked and asked for them to turn down their music. She was greeted by a torrent of abuse and threatened with violence. So panic stricken she called the police. When they arrived, they spoke with her then went up to see the lads who, just before the police arrived had turned the volume right down. The police, after talking to them came down and reassured her things would be OK now as, *they seem very reasonable and had agreed to keep their music much lower*. It was only a few minutes after the police had gone that she heard the lads banging on her door shouting, *You old grassing cow. Wait until we get our hands on you*. They eventually went back to their flat and back up went the music to full volume. She again phoned the police but as they drove up, they turned the volume back down. The police went and spoke to them again, but they denied everything, counter claiming that the woman was always having a go at them for nothing.

After that they made her life hell, banging on her door and swearing every time they passed. They watched her put her washing out and they came down and cut the line. They even threatened her home help who now had refused to call there. She was now petrified to phone the police and reluctantly told her son. He told me she'd kept it all from him as she knew he would go round and knowing their violent nature, she was concerned for his safety. He said, *Steve, there's three of them, if I go round, I'll go tooled up and end up in prison. I'm absolutely fuming. The police aren't doing anything and I just don't know what to do.*

I fuckin' do, kidda, you've just hired The A Team!

So usual detail, calls and texts were made and sent, pre-briefing pub was selected and all set for that Sunday. I didn't need too many men on this one as the small block of flats we were visiting was right in the middle of a group of houses. So, I was selective in who I contacted with the view to take a discrete elite squad of a dozen or so.

Well, that totally backfired. God only knows how everyone got word.

We met at the agreed pub and yeah, fuckin' loads turned up. I quickly gave the brief and got us off before more turned up.

As we got to the place, I noticed there seemed even more than what we had started with. When my man at the rear checked in, he told me people were still arriving and latching on to the tail of the convoy.

As we walked up to their door, I said, *Fuck, they're bound to of spotted us so let's just hope they answer the door, but I can't see it, otherwise we'll have to kick it in even though it will arouse too much attention.*

I knocked, and to my surprise one of them answered. Before I could open my mouth one of my men, Big Colin, who was by my side said, *Hiya, mate, we've come for the party*. The kid replied, with a stammer, *Party? There's no party here, mate*. Colin replied, *There fuckin' is now, matey*! And we pushed him up the stairs into his living room.

He was the only one there and I sat him down on a dining chair and began my lecture concerning their appalling behaviour with the old people in the flats and their treatment of my man's mother. I punctuated every word with a power slap. Halfway through the lecture I'd to change to his other cheek as the right-hand side one I'd been paying my attention to had turned into a complete mess of raw meat.

I concluded the speech with their leaving date. I gave them till the end of the week before they had to move out. I also told them the old folks there now had a direct hot line to me.

They actually left the following day.

We all drove back to the pub for a de-brief. As I got to the car park, I noticed lads carrying out of their cars items of furniture they'd nicked from the flat, one even had the telly away. It was probably all stolen in the first place, so I just smiled, turned away, and walked into the pub. One of the lads came to tell me it was rightful justice what had taken place there that night and the punishment was mild for the crime. I said, *Did you see the state of his face after I'd finished slapping him*, he said, *No, Steve, I was wedged in the kitchen. There were so many of us it got quite claustrophobic as more and more men kept surging up the stairs. We got forced into every fuckin' room, crammed into every space, at one point it got real scary.*

No, Steve, I couldn't see you, but we could all well fuckin' hear you. With that everyone broke into laughter.

Well, they fuckin' deserved it the horrible bastards. All the old people are now living happily ever after at the flats.

I LOVE IT WHEN A PLAN COMES TOGETHER…

UNITY – The Guild of the Brotherhood

Working the doors over the years I've collected a patchwork of scars and many hours of lost sleep through worry and anguish, but I wouldn't change a day of it. Mainly because of the golden quality of the friendship and the way you gel with the people you work with. People that stay lifelong loyal friends who remain there for each other inside and outside working hours and not just for the violent element of things but with the attraction and kudos of being part of a formidable mass. These people are there for each other in times of personal need, I know of no other profession like it.

I give here a few heart-warming examples to maybe illustrate this:

The Call-Outs to the Big Fights

These weren't exactly call-outs in the true sense of the word, they were more a gathering of the firm for a good cause.

One evening as I was working at The Foregate Bar a good friend of mine named Stevie Short came to see me. This kid is a very highly respected face throughout the North Wales coastline and major towns there. He came specially to tell me of a problem that was of a worrying concern to him. A promising young fighter they had up there had just split with his long-time girlfriend, a girl he'd been courting from school. The cow had left him for one of his friends. I instantly felt this kid's pain.

Stevie told me how he was just not coping and had turned to the bottle and God knows what else. He said, *We're all very worried now as we believe the kid is right on the edge.*

We've all tried talking to him but to no avail, you're our last chance, Steve, we think he'll probably listen to you, mate.

Yeah, Stevie, definitely, I said. *It's bank holiday Monday next week and we've got our Sunday get together night out. Make sure you bring him up.*

Every Monday Bank Holiday I arrange a full firm's night out on that Sunday as most of us won't be working and most will have Monday off to recover. It's kinda compulsory as I like to make sure we all stay in touch and meet up regularly on a social basis and not just for problems.

The lad he was referring to was a kid called Big Damo. A giant kick-boxer from North Wales. I'd met him a few times and you'd always see him on the call-outs and socials. He was a cracking polite courteous young man with good potential in his chosen sport of kick-boxing. On the Sunday, I approached the lad and listened to his story. Then I proceeded to have a right go at him. I made him aware that he'd been blessed with a God given talent that he was now throwing away. I tried to illustrate the wrongness of his actions by saying to him, *Damo, when you were born, that gift came to you, it could have gone to any of them, other babies born in that hospital that morning but it never, it came to you. The biggest sin for you would be to return that gift unwrapped.* He welled up a bit then gave me a hug and thanked me for the advice and taking time out for him. The rest of the night was good and then we all parted our separate ways.

It was a bit over a week later when I got a call from my good friend Russ Williams, the ex-world kick-boxing champ now turned coach, asking me what the fuck did I say to Damo, only he's been back in the gym and is now training every single day like a machine.

That phone conversation made my day, so I phoned Stevie up to discuss it. Steve said, *We're all up two Sunday's from now on our night out, I'll bring him up. I know he wants to see you as they're talking of giving him his first fight but don't say I mentioned it.* That said Sunday came, and we all met in one of our bars in town. Stevie came in with his lads with Damo at the back with a grin like the cat that had had it away with the cream. Stevie said, *I think Damo's got something he wants to ask you, mate,* and called him over.

He came over to me and said, *Hiya, boss, I don't know if you know but the last few weeks I've been in full training and Russ said if I continue the same, he's got me my first fight. It's in about four weeks.*

Absolute great news kidda, I said.

He said, *There's something else, boss.*

Yeah, go on, kidda, spit it out.

Well, Boss, would you do me the great honour of walking me to the ring.

Damo, I replied, *the honour would be all mine.*

I saw Stevie and said, *Let's get the whole firm out to this gig and give the lad a fuckin' good cheering section.* Stevie got all his North Wales lads who didn't need much prompting as Damo was a popular lad there. I'd put out the word to everywhere else and I too was met with the same response with Mick Francis as my special guest. Because of the potential numbers, I contacted the promoter who was a very good friend of mine named Phil, well he was at that time, but unfortunately a few years later we fell out badly over a sponsorship deal. However, I'd arranged to hook up with him. At our meeting I told him of the potential numbers and his eyes gaped open like fuckin' saucers. This man was the most money driven guy I've ever met. He would have his own grandmother fighting Mike Tyson to fill the card. I believe at that time he was the third biggest kick-boxing promoter in the country though he kept his profit mark-up very closely guarded usually crying poverty. We christened him *break-even*.

Phil, I said to him, *I want the full treatment as we'll have over a hundred men and I'll have Mick Francis with me, so I want something better than ringside*.

In honesty, Phil was a good man despite his few faults. That day he did us proud.

He told me to turn up after the first few preliminary fights had finished. He said to assemble in the pub just across from the venue and he would phone when to come over. The word I'd put out was it was to be an all in black gig, meaning the dress code was all black clothes. When we are all out together even socially, I like to make a statement, that night it most certainly did.

When I knew we were all assembled in the pub I began to hand out the tickets and collect in the money, there was well over a hundred of us and because of that number I managed to strike a good deal with Phil, (I think that was the toughest fight of the fuckin' night) and we all got a reduced rate from what the other ringside punters paid. At that time, I didn't know exactly how much of a brilliant deal we actually had got for our money.

While we were in the pub, I got the call off Phil to come over, he said he would personally meet us at the main door. I led us all out and over to the venue, the venue being the very large posh function room within the Chester racecourse. It was a huge place that hosted various gigs. As we got to the door, I saw Phil waiting for us and when he saw the actual number of us he couldn't contain his pleasure. He said he'd made special arrangements for us and for us to please follow him.

We walked around the side of the building to these large double emergency doors. He banged on the doors and they were opened up by two very scantily dressed ladies. Mick and I were in front but then these two ladies stepped in front of us and led us to our seats. As the doors were opened, two bright lights came on. Not like we needed any more attention on us as every person in the place (which was a couple of thousand), were looking over at this black army of men being ushered over to our seats like royalty. There had been a walkway pre-prepared to our seating arrangements which the girls were leading us over to. Well, when I say seating arrangements, when I saw where they were taking us, I thought I was dreaming. Phil had mounted a massive platform right off the back of the ring that rose up at the back to give us all perfect viewing with rows of nice seats. There was a deep banner all the way around it saying *Private, Steve Young, Loc 19 Guests Only*. What a fuckin' entrance, there was a preliminary fight still going on, but all eyes were on us. We all took our seats and the girls made us aware that we had our own private lounge bar just off from the stand where there were several other girls dressed similar to them who would provide waitress service for us. There were door staff at the entrance to our bar and two at the entrance to our VIP stand. What fantastic treatment. It was a damn good card too! There were a couple of national titles being fought for and the top billing was a European title.

Just before the fight, I got the call to go to Russ's changing room as Damo was next on. When I got there, Damo was in full flow smashing some pads one of the trainers was holding. We then got a knock on the door to say we were on. Russ then gave me my instructions. He said, *Steve, it's quite an entrance. We walk out to the top of these large stairs that sweep down into the hall and we walk right through the hall and to the ring.* He said he would walk a few paces in front then I would be next with Damo, his hands on my shoulders with the corner team following closely behind. *Will ya be OK with that, mate? Yeah, Russ, piece a cake,* I replied.

I hadn't noticed the other fighters making their entrance as I was busy sorting everyone out.

We came out of the changing room and got to the top of the stairs where we came into full view of the crowd. A bright spotlight beamed on us and Damo's entrance music belted out. Russ paused there for a few seconds then he made his way down. As instructed, I let him walk on a few paces then we followed. The noise of the crowd was deafening and every hair on the back of my neck was ridged. As we got nearer to the ring, we came into full view of our stand and the noise took the roof off.

Damo wasn't top billing on the card, but he was seen as the star of the show. We got to the edge of the ring and Russ got up and walked a few steps along the ropes. I got up and stood at the near side of them, we both put a foot on the second rope and pulled up on the third rope as Big Damo climbed through, with still ear damaging cheers, and chants of *Da-mo Da-mo.*

Although the opponent was a very credible fighter, Damo smashed him to fuckin' jam in two rounds. As the win was officially announced, I presented him with his trophy. He then give me a hug that lifted me off the ground and nearly broke my whole rib cage.

It was a finale to a great night. Afterwards, we went back to our nightclub in town where they had kept the VIP room private for us. I made a short speech congratulating him on the way he'd turned his life around and his great victory that night. We all toasted him with champagne then proceeded to all get abso-fuckin-lutely shit faced! The nice epilogue to this story is that Damo went on to have several other fights before crossing over to orthodox boxing where he has started to climb in the ranking. As this book goes to print, he is Welsh amateur heavyweight champion. Every fight we've supported him and will continue to do so.

I think there's a parable in this story for all of us…

Times of Grief

As I've already said, this job is like no other profession. The way the lads compromise their own safety and put their necks on the line for each other inside and outside of work. We have always been there for each other in the good times like with Damo and the bad times, like turning to on the shouts, and also in times of sadness like the loss of a loved one.

At my father's funeral, myself and my family left with the hearse from Dad's house at 10 a.m. All the other mourners had arranged to meet at his local pub which was just around the corner. The landlord, who was a great friend of my dad's, had opened up the pub for them and served free tea and coffee.

Unbeknown to me, arrangements had been made for the hearse and our following limousines to pause at the pub. As we got near, I could see the large crowd of people waiting there. We waited for everyone to get into their cars and to fall in behind us. Mick Francis took up lead car in front of the hearse in his black Range Rover which really looked the part with a black flag mounted on the top. The church was a couple of miles down a lovely country lane. As we got there, I noticed a lot of other mourners waiting outside the church, I wondered why they hadn't gone in. We parked a good way from the church where we were kept waiting in the limousines. I was becoming confused until the door was opened. As we got out, I saw two lines of men from the hearse up through the church gates, up the pathway, and right up to the church doors. It was all the lads, all dressed in black, forming a guard of honour. We carried the coffin through this cordon followed by my family and the rest of the mourners. After the service they again took up their position from the church to the grave then after the burial, they reformed from the church out to the car park. It touched everyone and I personally can't remember feeling as proud and honoured. We all went back to the little local pub where I made a short speech thanking friends and family but made particular reference to my unique, special adopted family which brought on a standing round of applause and me to tears … One other funeral of note was the sad passing of Mick's father.

I got the call to go up to Manchester for a meeting with Mick and his brother and they asked me to take charge of the procession management and security arrangements. It was a very high honour but a huge responsibility as he told me the procession was to take quite a long route around where he lived.

After the initial meeting we had arranged a full planning meet with the funeral director and Mick to discuss the route and all other finer details.

On that next meet, I took up my friend and business partner, Gaz. With his university degree I knew he would be a great asset when planning something like this involved.

We all met at Mick's office where we discussed and planned out the route. We then all got in Mick's Range Rover and drove the route as Gaz sketched drawings and made notes. It was a bloody good move me taking him up. When we got home, we spent the rest of the night transferring his rough sketches onto the computer. The route of the procession was quite long and crossed some main areas of Manchester where traffic would need holding up. We realised then it was going to take a lot of men to pull this one off successfully.

So, the very same detail as a call-out, I put out the shout. I then called a meeting with eight of my senior men who were nominated as team leaders. Each would be taking control of a party of men. The plan was every time the procession came to a road junction my men would be there holding up the traffic until it passed. We had planned it to have at least three junctions ahead ready manned at any one time. Each team leader had his own map of the route with his junctions highlighted. They each had a nominated driver, and the separate groups would be sorted out on the morning, hopefully we would get a good turn-out. We did…

On the morning, a lot of us met at mine where we had a photo taken. We looked really smart all in black with black ties. I had the picture mounted in a large frame with a plaque under the photo with all our signatures which I later presented to Mick.

So, we set off from mine and headed off to Mick's father's house in Moss Side, Manchester where the hearse and procession was to leave from with a couple of stops to pick up other groups. As we got to the house I parked up on this large grassy island opposite the house and checked in with the funeral director as Gaz drove off with the lads to take up their positions. I was to be the lead vehicle in my big new shiny black Nissan pick-up which I'd fixed two black flags to, and I stuck two large *Loc 19* stickers on the back, it so very much looked the part. What I hadn't realised was that it had been raining and where I'd parked it was quite boggy. In my car were my driver and two back-up map readers. As we got in to take up our position the extra weight sunk us deeper into the mud. My driver, Jo, started up the car but even with the four-wheel drive it just kept skidding and sinking further. I started getting stressed and began to rant and rave, banging on the dashboard shouting, *Get the fuckin' thing on the road for fuck's sake.* This wasn't having the right effect as in panic, my driver floored the accelerator and drove us deeper into the mud. Everyone in the car was trying to calm me down as it wasn't exactly the correct behaviour for a funeral. Then I got a knock on the door, it was Martin one of Mick's senior men. He was covered in mud, he shouted, *What ya doing, ya mad bastard*? then he pointed to his car it was a light blue Rolls Royce, I'd covered it in mud and large sods of turf and not only his car but several other mourners' cars too. We sheepishly crept out and changed cars.

That was the only fuck-up on the day as everything after went with military precision. Every junction was covered as we approached, every time we passed through one, the lads would then take another route outside of the procession to get to their next location. As we got to the church, I held up the hearse and the mourners until all the men got there and into the guard of honour position. After the service, the hearse and mourners went on to the burial which was a few miles from there. We had all taken up our positions with exactly the same detail.

We had pulled it off. It was a perfect operation. I was in constant radio contact with all the cars via walkie-talkie. I'd set the pace of the cortège while Gaz was scooting round controlling things on the ground. Afterwards, Mick, his family, and nearly all the mourners thanked us for making the day special. We were invited to the hotel where a buffet was being laid on, but I declined on behalf of us all as I could see we would attract a lot of attention and that wasn't what the day was meant to be about. So, we all got off and drove to this lovely county restaurant near where I live. One of the girls with us asked the barmaid if we could push a few tables together to seat us all which she agreed saying, *Just give me the number of the end table for when I make out your bill.* She looked at the table number and shouted, *It's 19.* We all looked in shock then all burst into laughter as we all walked over to examine it. A few of us, me included, took a photo of it on our mobiles as we were all sure no one would believe the coincidence.

This is how our profession used to function. We were always there for each other, in times of danger, sadness, or troubles.

Sadly, I don't see this happening with these new large, modern door companies. That's all they are now mostly, just another fuckin' business.

The Shout of the Big Mistake

It was late one Saturday evening when I received a call from the head doorman at the large nightclub, I had several lads on. He told me of a bad incident they'd just suffered. A group of lads off the Lache, one

of the large estates in town, had been fighting with some lads from out of town. Our lads had stopped the fight and separated them. He told me they put the local lads out the front door and at that point they were fine. They held onto the other party then put them out the rear exit so as not to let the two parties meet up again and go for round two. The local lads were hanging around the front waiting for the other crew to be put out. Things then started to get hostile as the local lads wanted to know why the other crew weren't getting put out. The doormen didn't want to tell them they were getting put out the back as they knew full well they would go round and weigh them in, and in the mood they were in, there would have been some serious casualties. So as best they could, they kept trying to move them on, but to no avail. The head doorman went on to say that instead of moving on they were on their phones enlisting back-up. He told me that as their numbers started to swell, they tried to breach the door. They eventually had to lock the doors for their own safety. It was at the end of the night and they put the last of the customers out of a side door still keeping the front doors locked as by this time they'd started to kick the doors and were hurling anything they could find at the large windows. It was like the whole club was under siege and although several calls were made, there was no sign of the police. They eventually dispersed but not without issuing some serious threats to the doormen. The head doorman was extremely worried over the threatened comeback of all this with one major concern. One of our lads worked in a garage right in the middle of their estate. He was certain they would give him a visit on Monday on his return to work. The kid needed his job and was worried he'd be unable to continue working there.

I was furious they'd kicked off on our lads knowing full well they were my men and causing a fight. Then they made phone calls to bring out the troops and held the place under siege. I was straight on the case and called an emergency shout for that following night which was a Sunday.

We all met in one of our bars in town to have the pre-brief. Although it was short notice, we had a damn good turn-out.

The plan was to give their local pub a visit and hopefully capture some of the offending gentlemen and read them the riot act.

I gave the usual pre-brief then off we drove in usual convoy detail.

When the last vehicle had checked in, we all got out of our cars and slowly filed into the pub. There was only a hand full of people in the place and none who were part of last night's crew, but, as I've already mentioned, that wasn't a problem as it actually works in your favour once the Chinese whispers get going.

I asked to speak to the landlord and explained what had gone on and why we were there. He and the few punters that were in the pub went white with shock. I told the landlord that if there was a repeat performance, we would be making house calls next time.

We all slowly filed out and into our vehicles. We did a slow tour of the estate then headed back to the bar in town for a post-brief.

No sooner had I got home, my phone never stopped. People from that estate wanting to know what the hell was that all about. Every time I explained I was met with, *No, you must have it all wrong.* Eventually, I received a call from a man called Joe, he kinda ran things there and was a controlling voice. He said, *Steve, what the fuck was all that about tonight.* I again explained how the lads had kicked off on some out-of-towners, then turned on us, held the place to siege, and worst of all called a call-out and summoned back-up from the estate. Joe said, *Steve, the lads wouldn't cross you like that, let me make some phone calls and get back to you.*

After only about half an hour he did. *Steve, you have it all totally wrong, them out-of-towners picked on our lads. If you remember, when you put our lads out, they went without trouble, but they felt a bit peeved as they'd been attacked and not retaliated. So, they were waiting for them to be put out. There was more of them other lads, so they were phoning some of the rest of their party who were in town but hadn't gone to the club, no way was it a call-out. Yeah, OK, they got a bit leery with your lads because they thought you had taken the other lot's side and had let them stay in.*

I said, *What about the threats to our man who works in the garage on your manor, they threatened death on him and to burn the place down.*

Joe explained how it was all said in drunken anger. A couple of them had taken some bad knocks off them other lot and were furious they'd got away with it and they were getting the blame. Now everyone here is worried what's going to happen next.

I felt like shit, I'd got it completely wrong, and it looked like I was taking the side of these out-of-town scum bags against the local kids.

I asked Joe if he would arrange a meet for the following day at the Queens Head, one of our large bars in town. The lads used the Queens Head when they came up town. I asked him to bring the main players of the party and any senor heads off the estate. He agreed and the meet was set for one o'clock the following day.

My driver picked me up the next afternoon and we set off to the meet. We stopped a few streets away and waited up.

It's always best to be a few minutes late on these things, it gives them time to get nerved up and dwell.

They phoned to say they'd arrived but would stay outside and only walk in when I arrived which was quite understandable.

We drove up and shook hands and I escorted them all in. It was a nice turn-out, there were a good few of the young lads and a few of the senior heads off that manor. I was just about to ask what everyone was drinking when the bar suddenly filled with police. There was a head inspector who grouped together the lads and took them outside leaving me and my driver there. We took up a seat by the window totally bemused. My driver stood up and looked out of the window and went white. He pointed for me to look. They had cut off the whole of the main street. It was flooded with police; they even had a chopper circling above. Me and my driver sat there frozen to the spot waiting to get tugged when in slips one of the lads. He said, *They're talking to Joe right now but, Steve, if it's OK with you, can I get off as I'm in breach of my bail condition coming here.* I said, *Yes, kidda*, and got my driver to show him out the back where there's a series of alleyways where he could make his escape. We shook hands and I thanked him for coming even though it was at risk to himself. He smiled and said, *I wasn't expecting this much attention*. We laughed nervously and we got him off.

After a while, the lads came back into the bar and took up seats around our table, the police remaining outside. Joe said, *Who the fuck do they think you are, Steve, Al Capone*? I asked what had gone on. He told me, *The head copper seemed to know everything and asked me what was going on here today. I told him it was just a social visit to town with a few mates, but he knew everything. He said, I know exactly what's taking place, there was an incident at Brannigans on Saturday night with people off your estate, then last night a very large group of men visited your local pub and your estate. Now you've come here for a meeting*. Joe told me he was amazed on how much he knew. He then went on to say that the copper said, as he pointed at me through the window, *That man in there is a very dangerous man, we can't usually deal with him when he comes out like this but today, we're ready. You've walked right into the lion's den and you could get butchered in there today. Like I said, we can't usually deal with him but today we're ready and can assure your safe passage back*. Joe said, *I told them, yes, we were here for a private pre-arranged meeting and unless that was against the law, we're going back in to attend it.*

I said, *Nice one, Joe*. I ordered the drinks and we sat down to talk with the police still outside watching on.

I said to the young lads, *Look, lads, these clubs and bars in town are for you the locals, the lads from round here, not primarily for out-of-towners. If we ever have any trouble, I expect you all to be behind us as back-up, fighting with us*. They all smiled and nodded. Joe then said, *That's great, Steve, everyone is waiting to hear what's been said here today and they'll be made up with that.*

I reassured them that no one was barred, and we all shook hands and left. Later that afternoon I got a call from Joe, he said, *The young lad who had breached his bail and tried to get off got captured and they had to go and bail him out from the cop shop on the way home. As we were waiting the inspector called me into his office and demanded to know what had gone on at the meeting. I told him that all the police had ever done for our community is chase the kids around the estate, that man today in only half an hour has done more for our young lads than your lot has ever done, so unless you're going to arrest us, we're off. Was that OK for you, Steve*?

Yeah, Joe, very nicely said, thank you.

I told him anything I can help you or the lads with in the future he should contact me.

I felt twenty foot tall knowing I'd been of some help to an area that in my opinion gets greatly overlooked.

That feeling of elation soon passed as I was very soon made aware of how badly I was now being seen by the police. I started to realise how I must have been pissing them off all these years with all the shouts over issues they should have been left to deal with. I thought I was doing good, I never once made the first move or fired the first shot, I only ever responded, sometimes only after two or three repeated attacks or call-outs were aimed at us.

What you have to remember is the police are the biggest gang on the block, a lot of people forget to respect that fact.

Since then, they've opposed our company when quoting for new venues and I suppose from what they perceive of me, they're right.

We still do a good few places in town and neighbouring towns mostly where the place is privately owned and the proprietor has a vested interest in the proper safety of the place and himself as we're the most effective firm there is here.

If I had my time over again, I wonder if in the long run it might have been better if I had have left the police to deal with some of the problems I got involved with. It's just that on a lot of shitty issues their hands were tied, mine weren't. It was never my intention to be in opposition to them. I just wish there may have come a time the police saw us as someone doing very nearly the same job – dealing with cunts…

CHAPTER FIVE

Getting at the Bollocks

There have been many humorous, mischievous pranks-come-practical-jokes we pulled over the years in times of revenge or purely out of latent childish naughtiness. I truly believe in the saying, *the Devil makes work for idle hands …* He did with us!

Looking back, I cannot believe we got up to such outrageous pranks. Nevertheless, I thought some that are printable were worthy to recall.

Gary's Fishing Gadgets

One evening when I was working at The Foregate Club, I had the misfortune to encounter the most arrogant, pompous, condescending woman I've ever met. This woman was so far up herself I'm surprised she could breathe. She turned up at the door in jeans and at that time we had a *no denim* dress code in place. I politely refused her entry explaining the reason. She instantly exploded on me in vile condemnation. *Don't be ridiculous, you stupid man. How dare you refuse me entry?* I again explained we had a strict dress code, and her jeans were contravening that policy. She became more and more verbally hostile. I explained to her that it would show unfair discrimination on my part if I allowed her to come in as I'd refused quite a few other people wearing denim that evening. But it all seemed to go right over her head as she replied, *How dare you criticise my clothes, you, you're just a bouncer. Do you know I was chairing a very high-powered meeting today at work and now I'm being told I can't go into a bar to meet my friends by a bouncer who probably doesn't have two brain cells to rub together.*

I tried to put it to her that her job wasn't the issue here it was the dress code, something the manager had put in place not me, but she was having none of it. She was so outraged that someone as low in the food chain as a doorman could have the audacity to point out that her attire was incorrect for the venue.

I could feel myself getting more and more worked up and I started to worry I might say or do something I would regret later, so I did something I very seldom do and relented. I said, *Look, OK, calm down, go in and find your friends, explain what's happened, I don't mind if you have one quick drink but don't take advantage of my lenience and be brief as I've explained, we can't allow you to stay in there*. On hearing this she completely erupted shouting, *How dare you tell me where I can and cannot go, you insolent lout.*

With this, I put my hands both side of her shoulders and moved her to the side of the door saying, *Fine. If you don't want to come in, move out of the way of the other customers who do*. She immediately got on her phone and called the police claiming she'd been assaulted. The police turned up but took no action as it had all been picked up on the street CCTV and also the manager had witnessed it all.

The following night, as I got to work, the manager met me to tell me that the horrible slag had contacted his area manager to lodge a complaint. They took it seriously until he told them that I had his and the police's full backing on it. So, the area manager sent her a polite letter explaining as much.

The following week as I arrived for work, I could see the manager at the door. He was holding a newspaper and smiling. I asked him why he was smirking, and he opened the newspaper to show me an article in the *Have Your Say* page of the local rag. I read with disbelief as that horrible witch had written a slanderous false account of the whole incident, describing how this brain-dead bouncer (OK that bit might be true) was trying to have an aggressive power trip with this little defenceless female who was reduced to tears. The fuckin bitch had tried every avenue to get me sacked but each time the truth prevailed so now she resorted to public character assassination.

Although we all laughed and found it pitiful, I was quietly fuming. This stuck-up whore was hell bent to have me made aware of my low-life position in comparison to her superior class and breeding.

I walked over to where Gary was working and showed him the article and he too was angered at it but then he smiled and said, *We can have the last laugh here, Dig,* and he pointed to the top of the article where she'd put her name AND her address.

He said, *We'll just have to give her house a little visit tomorrow night after work.* He said he would pick up some fishing gadgets in the day. *Don't worry, Dig, I've done this many times. Fishing gadgets*, I thought.

I never questioned him on that, obviously it was some kind of gangster slang.

The following night after we finished work, I got in his car and we set off to the address. We arrived at the house. Gary said, *Great, just one small car on the drive, that's got to be hers. She must live alone*. I thought, *yep, I can understand that*. We stealthily crept out of the car then out of the boot he passed me one of two sealed plastic buckets. *Come on, Dig, you go the other side of her car.*

What are they, Gary? I asked.

He whispered, *Fishing gadgets, Dig. I only found out about a couple of years ago that you could buy them like this over here.*

I opened up the lid and it was full of maggots; he'd been to a fuckin' fishing tackle shop and bought about six pints of maggots. I said, *What the fuck are we going to do with these*? He said, *Watch*! As we crept up to the car, he began feeding them through the vent grill on the top of the bonnet. *Get the other side, Dig, and do that side*. I could hardly contain my laughter as he whispered that they make their way through into the cabin and a couple of days later you have a constant hatch of ten thousand blue bottles for weeks.

I remembered picking my son up from fishing once and just a small handful of maggots had spilt in the boot and yeah for weeks after I'd had big lazy blue bottles mingin out the cabin of my car that seem to come alive every time I started the engine. I thought with glee what would six to eight pints of the fuckers be like.

Hey, it couldn't have happened to a nicer person!!!

The Green Shoots of Spring

I'll have to be careful here so as not to incriminate us or anyone else, so these next few paragraphs are penned with a cloak of anonymity.

One evening, this horrible bastard off one of the local estates who I'll refer to as Person X had been caught on police CCTV getting refused entry at one of the clubs in town due to his violent, aggressive behaviour. The police CCTV had warned every venue of this man. So everywhere he tried to get into he was refused. He started to make his way into the main drag of town where the bars were manned by the top door company and ran by an exceedingly handsome gentleman who I'll refer to as Person A. As Person X was walking towards one of the bars the lads shook their heads at him and at first, he seemed to acknowledge this and went to walk by. Then, without warning, he spun around and smashed one of the doormen right in the face with what seemed to be a rock or half house brick then sped off into the crowd. The doorman's face was in quite a bad way and needed hospital treatment.

The police arrived and took statements and retrieved footage of the incident from their CCTV. They then went straight to Person A the handsome boss of that firm. Person A had already been made aware of the incident. The police told him not to get involved and leave it to them as they were sure it would have all been picked up very clearly on camera and they'd started their investigations.

Person A informed them he'd started his own investigations and by the end of the night he'd have Person X's fuckin' shoe size, (which he did).

The following night Person A was contacted by the police again as they too had gathered all the relevant information and had made an arrest. They informed Person A that the kid was now out on police bail and to just leave matters to the authorities. *The kid's got form and he'll get a nice long holiday from it.* They reminded Person A that any revenge missions would jeopardise all this. So Person A sat on his hands and waited for the slow wheels of our justice system to turn.

Eventually the case came to court and would you just believe it, the horrible twat got a suspended sentence. I thought if we'd have hit him half as bad, brick or no brick, we would be on a long one.

So, OK, Person A had been patient and waited to see how the justice system performed and as half suspected, it was badly lacking.

So, Person A puts together a small elite squad. They capture Person X. He gets the good slapping he originally deserved then accidentally all his clothes came off and his hands and his feet somehow got fastened together with heavy duty zip ties. Then strangely the ties on the hands and the ties around his feet got fastened together positioning him in a very bent over pose. He then somehow or other got shackled to some nearby railings in that extremely bent over, nude position. Then, as if by magic, a bunch of daffodils got inserted up the poor chap's bottom. The poor lamb was left there like that for all to see.

I believe this took place early hours of the morning and he got rescued sometime during morning rush hour. I was surprised no Good Samaritan rescued him earlier, though by all accounts, he was a very much disliked person. I actually heard people were taking photos of him on their mobiles.

Yep, after a long hard winter a nice show of spring flowers always raises the spirits, don't you think?

It Does What It Says on the Tin

One night when I was working at The Foregate Club I was signing in and noticed a Post-it pad. While no one was looking I whizzed it and took it with me to the front door. As some of the first customers were coming in, I started writing dodgy things on it and sticking it onto people's backs. It was well funny, but after a short time they would fall off. The following night one of the other doormen, who'd thought it was that funny, had bought a pad of those fluorescent sticky stars that café and chip shops use to write special offers on and stick on their windows or walls.

They worked a fuckin' treat.

Absolutely infantile I know, but it was funny as fuck to see a real classy bird dressed to the nines walking around with a fluorescent sign on their back saying *Shag Me*. Or a poncey Brad Pitt look-alike dude with *I've just farted stuck* on the back of his Armani suit.

Some of these fuckers must have been chrome-plated cunts as we'd often see them coming out at the end of the night with them still on, their mates saying nothing.

We had to knock it on the head in the end as the manager was spending most of the following day apologising to people.

A Nice Green Salad to Come Home To

So as not to incriminate anyone here, I'll just say I'm aware of another shady prank concerning someone who crossed us in a shitty disloyal way.

This man really had to be dealt with, but when he was visited, very conveniently he and his slut of a wife had got off on holiday for two weeks. His house was cased up and found to be of easy access. So a few evenings later the house was infiltrated. The lads were not there to rob or trash the place, but were armed with buckets, liquid plant food, pressure hoses, and dozens of bags of salad cress seeds. First, they mixed the plant food with water in the buckets, then transferred the cocktail into the pressure hose containers, primed the containers then hosed it everywhere. The three-piece suite, the curtains, the carpets, on the bed, even the bleedin' wallpaper, then cast, scattered and dabbed the seeds in a very generous manner. I can remember doing this at school on blotting paper with just water to great effect.

One of the lads looked in after a couple of days to see green shoots sprouting everywhere. God only knows what kind of cress jungle they came home to … He he he…

CONCLUSION

It saddens me to see how the job is now functioning after much interference. It is now strictly regulated by a government body called the SIA. Now you need to apply for a door supervisor's badge. For this you have to go on one of their induction courses which can cost up to £300. Then you pay £200 for one of their application forms, from that you will be vetted by these people and they will do a complete police search. The only qualification you need to get one of these badges off these fuckers in their ivory tower is to have a clean police record. They're not in the least concerned if you can protect people's sons and daughters from cunts and bullies and be able to cope with modern-day violence or to have the know-how and the experience to read verbal and non-verbal pre-fight indicators.

In my day, if you stood on a door you had to be, and look to be, harder than anyone that entered your venue. You had to be able to do it, you needed street cred, and to hold respect, all of which acted as a deterrent in most cases of violence, but the times where it didn't, you would deal with them. Doormen used to be an exceptionally different breed: harder and tougher than the average man. They were usually pro boxers, top martial artists, or local hard men. You were in a violent job and to coin a phrase off another famous doorman, Geoff

Thompson, *If you're dealing with shit, you've got to have someone who can shovel.*

They're handing out these badges to school leavers, squirts totally unprepared no marks who see it as a career move to getting into girl's knickers.

I'm a second-degree black belt, I do a doorman's course for our lads about four times a year. I call it the *Minimum Injury Ejection Techniques* course. I've done them for more than fifteen years. I used to do them with Gary Spiers all around the country. I teach techniques that work, techniques that get nasty twats out in one piece without you getting hurt in the process. It keeps the lads out of court and more importantly, out of hospital.

Mick Francis asked if he could sit in on one of the courses. He was so impressed he commissioned me to take all his men. He gave me twenty men at a time which I took over three weekends, the sessions lasting two hours. It took me months to complete. I got many phone calls, texts, and letters off these lads and still do, usually after they've used one of the techniques to good effect.

Mick Francis put me on a course to qualify me to be able to take the SIA induction course, which I passed and started delivering to potential doormen as part of the prerequisite to applying for their badge. I mentioned to the lady who ran the company who took me for the course that I strongly believed that the students should also be given some kind of basic training in safe ejection techniques and I would be more than willing to have some input in this. She told me that the SIA was in the process of formulating such a course and I would be called back to take this and deliver it on the back of the induction course.

Well, a few weeks later I was called back to take this new instructor's course, it was called *Physical Intervention* and was a week-long course.

The first morning I walked in and was met by this skinny grey-faced man. He started by introducing himself as an ex-copper with no experience of nightclub security. He told us the course had been commissioned by the government and put together by them and the police. He went on to explain that the whole emphasis was on teaching *none pain inducing techniques*.

None pain inducing techniques? What the fuck is that, I thought, *fuckin' hypnosis*?

We all had to introduce ourselves and from the point of my introduction saying I'd been a martial arts instructor and had been taking courses in ejection techniques for many years, he took an instant dislike to me.

I managed to suffer through the week of the absolute crap he was peddling with the thought that I would put some of my teachings along with it when I was delivering it. But it was unbelievably hard to keep quiet, I was often at bursting point wanting to shout out, *You fucking clueless prick, you're teaching shit that will get people fuckin' hurt* but I managed to contain myself.

On the Friday was the exam, we all had to demonstrate one of the moves. The technique I was given was called the *Hook and Turn*. This was meant to be a rescuing manoeuvre, assisting your partner from an attacker strangling him. It was so pathetic you couldn't even laugh at it. It went something like this. Someone was strangling your colleague, so you had to calmly walk behind the attacker, hook his left shoulder with your left hand formed in a hook shape and pull. With your other hand you pushed his other shoulder, twist him round and push him towards the door. Yeah, like that would fuckin' work with an eighteen stone nasty cunt with ten pints of larger down his neck and six grams of beak up his nose. Yeah, I can just see it, *Yeah, OK, mate, that's a fair one, I'll fuck off then*. What world do these people live in?

I wanted to say to this clueless fucker, *Come work with me this weekend and test drive that one out*. But I bit my tongue and demo'd it as was shown. At the end of all the demonstrations, he told everyone they had passed but took me to one side to inform me I'd failed. I couldn't believe it. I had more experience than any of the others there, but he told me little bits of my demonstration were out and that I was, and looked, too scary to be giving these courses. He believed I would be off putting to students taking it.

I drove home in a complete daze. How could this man qualify to even be in the same room as me let alone teach me shit all week then fail me on it?

So now you have the SIA who prevent the best men working the job and fuckers going around teaching unprepared student doormen dangerous, unworkable shit.

Yes, maybe I'm a dinosaur about ready to become extinct with the rest of my kind, but I'm so glad I had my time when I did. I've worked with some great men, absolute warriors, and made some genuine true friends who were prepared to put their neck on the line for each other inside and outside work.

What other profession can you say that about?

Printed in Great Britain
by Amazon

86560967R00116